WHO WANTS TO BE ME?

ALSO BY RECIS PHILBIN:

I'm Only One Man!

Entertaining with Regis & Kathie Lee

Cooking with Regis & Kathie Lee

WHO WANTS TO BE ME?

Regis Philbin
with Bill Zehme

HYPERION

New York

791.45
PHI

This book is for my Joy.

If you think living my life has been stressful, how about living with this
stress because you're married to me?

She was minding her own business, having a great time, in fact—and
then I came into her life with all my misadventures.

They say for better or worse . . . Well, she made it
so much better for me.

I can't imagine getting through it without her.

Are You Ready FOR THIS?

The night of the 2000 Daytime Emmy Awards was a classic.
A classic for me, anyway.

Could have been a Jack Lemmon movie, really.

Appropriately enough, it was five years ago this very night when I finished my last book, *I'm Only One Man!* I devoted the final pages to the usual Emmy night scenario, the one I had come to know so well. Oprah had just won again. Joy and I were walking out of the theater, threading our way through the raucous crowd. People were yelling; people were cheering. It was over—I had lost the Emmy.

AGAIN.

In fact, Kathie Lee and I have lost in our talk-show category so many times, I just stopped going to the ceremony a few years ago. Why bother? It used to be a Phil Donahue lock every year. Then, once in a while, Joan Rivers or Sally or Montel would sneak in. And, of course, Oprah has won so many Emmys, she finally begged off by taking herself out of the running. And now Rosie O'Donnell has won three in a row.

Anyway, when you work every day, weekends become very special to you—especially New York weekends in May. So I decided to pass on these tedious Friday nights of being locked in a theater for three hours with a camera aimed at your face, just itching to get your disappointed reaction when you don't win again.

I don't even know which of our *Live!* shows Gelman—our indefatigable executive producer—has handed in for judgment over the years. Frankly, I wish he'd stop trying. But this year was different. Because, yes, this was the year of *Who Wants to Be a Millionaire*—the show that changed the face of prime-time network television. Made it important again. So, naturally, the show got nominated for an Emmy—and, lo and behold, I got nominated for best host of a game show. The only wrinkle was it would be part of the Daytime Emmys. Something about an old rule that a game show must always be judged in the Daytime Emmy category. I know it doesn't make sense, but the committee didn't have the time to change the rules. Or something like that.

Naturally, the expectations around the *Millionaire* set were running high and optimistic. It's really something to start up a new show, with all of its potential pitfalls—and then watch it go to the top of the charts and stay there. What a thrill for all of us!

And now these nominations. How could I not go this year?

I had, of course, given up on *Live! With Regis & Kathie Lee*, but *Millionaire* might be something different. Besides, the staff and the crew had poured their hearts into this new venture—

I HAD TO BE THERE!

Frankly, I thought maybe even *Live!* might have a chance—this being Kathie Lee's last year and our final nomination together. I was thinking: Maybe this could be the year. The last chance. The final thank-you for all those mornings we met behind the desk, live, with no writers and made something out of nothing—and, sometimes, something out of *something*—and gave those nine o'clock viewers a laugh to get their day started. For fifteen years, eleven of them in national syndication, we had met, walking that tightrope of live, spontaneous conversation without a net under us. We had weathered all the fads, as morning TV sank into the sewer of slimy sex, set-up confrontations between family members and, eventually, fistfights between ex-lovers.

Those shows came in like gangbusters—got all the attention of the media. And we just plugged along with our "Well-what-did-you-do-last-night?" And now, as we wrapped up fifteen years together, we were still right up there with the daytime leaders. Through the years we had even spawned other shows. As we took vacations, our replacements had a chance to strut their stuff. They had every chance to shine on a show that was up and running. So George Hamilton and Howie Mandel and Leeza Gibbons and Suzanne Somers and Marilu Henner got their shots. Some made it, some didn't. And then there was Rosie—a natural-born force if ever there was one. She just had to succeed—she couldn't miss. But even Rosie had to pinch-hit for Kathie Lee three times before the programming geniuses saw the light.

Yes, the more I thought about it, the more I thought that this fantasy could happen—

MAYBE WE COULD WIN AFTER ALL.

Three weeks earlier, on the night of the annual Correspondents Dinner in Washington, D.C., Pat Sajak—one of the most consistent nominees for best game-show host—came over to my table. Quite seriously, he said, "It's yours this year—I'm not even going." A week later, as I kept hearing more of the same, Joy said, "I've got to find a special dress. This is going to be a very special night for you. . . ."

Despite all this, I still remembered: This is the daytime Emmys where anything can happen.

That week, my *Millionaire* executive producer, Michael Davies, was more than his ebullient self. He was supremely optimistic. Even Gelman—battered as we were by all the consecutive losses—seemed to sense that *this might be the year.* . . .

That night, Joy was looking glamorous in her new dress as we stepped from the limo onto that carpet in front of Radio City Music Hall. Fans were roaring my name from the sidewalk on Fifty-first Street. They sensed it, too.

Fran Weinstein, the New York field producer for *Entertainment Tonight*—and a former producer of mine—came toward me with microphone in hand, camera crew rolling behind her. I swear to God—*I thought I saw a little tear in her eye!* She said, "This is your night!"

I told her, "I think it's gonna be Donny and Marie! How long can the Academy keep those two waiting?"

We laughed.

And then it was Shaun Robinson from *Access Hollywood:* "How do you feel? You got your speech ready?"

My God, I thought, *they really think I'm going to win!*

On top of that, our seats this year were better than ever—right up front, next to the stairs that led up to the stage. A good omen. In years gone by, they put us so far over to one side, we were up against the wall of Radio City. I used to listen to the traffic go by outside on Fiftieth Street.

Then, the multi-winning host of *Jeopardy!*, Alex Trebek, came over and said, "It's all yours this year—congratulations!" Yes, even Trebek had put away thoughts of our imaginary little feud and was very generous.

Suddenly, more than ever, I started to really fight the feeling that I was going to win.

Don't take it for granted, I kept telling myself.

Anyway, right away, the best talk-show award went again to Rosie's show. That was not a good sign for us. Usually best show and best host are synonymous. Then came the talk-show host category—and, naturally, there came that flicker of hope. Joy was on one side of me, Kathie Lee on the other, Frank beside her. We all held hands . . . but it didn't help.

Yes, it was Rosie again, for the fourth straight time.

And why not? She deserves it.

As she walked by us she shot an almost embarrassed look that said, "Sorry . . ."

Don't worry, Rosie—

WE'VE HAD A LOT OF PRACTICE AT THIS!

But now we're up to the best game show competition—and, sure enough, it went to the *Millionaire* show! And there was Michael Davies, resplendent in his grandfather's Scottish dress pants—whatever they're called—receiving the award and saying: *"Regis Philbin—you are a god!"*

Easy, Michael, easy!

And there were my supporting supervising producers, among them Vincent Rubino, who had started with me on *Live!* as a college intern and worked his way up to being one of our top associate producers before striking out on his own. I said to Gelman, "Isn't it funny? Our Vinnie 'Boombatz' has now won an Emmy before we have!"

Finally, the moment arrived—the best game-show host category. A. Martinez and Jackie Zeman, costars on *General Hospital,* were the presenters. They read the list of nominees—and, by God, the audience roared at the mention of my name! It was a *Millionaire* crowd all the way.

Could this really be happening?

Was I finally gonna win one of these things?

Joy clutched my hand.

ALL RIGHT, I WAS NERVOUS, IF YOU CAN IMAGINE THAT!

Jackie opened the envelope and haltingly announced—

"It's a tie."

A TIE!?

The crowd murmured in disbelief.

Then she announced that Bob Barker was one of the winners. He wasn't there—he was home convalescing after knee surgery. Bob Barker, one of the princes of daytime television, still there with *The Price is Right,* like he's been all these years.

So who was the other one?

She stepped back.

She was having a little trouble reading it.

A few people in the balcony screamed—*"REGIS!"*

The crowd was on edge.

A. Martinez took the paper and calmly announced that the other winner was . . .

Tom Bergeron of *Hollywood Squares.*

There was a gasp in the room.

A loud gasp.

At least, that's what people told me later.

Tom, a young pro at talk and game shows, had pulled off an upset. He bounded up onstage and looked right at me, then shrugged his shoulders as if to say, "I don't get it." And he actually did say, "I thought I was coming here just for the dinner." He was very gracious up there.

But the other Emmy had slipped away.

We finally went home.

Did we talk on the way?

I don't remember.

But when we got home there was a telegram from California sent by my good friends Barry and Susan Glazer. They were congratulating me on winning the Emmy. And, believe it or not, there was even a beautiful congratulatory watch from Fred the Jeweler in Beverly Hills. These California people—always on my side. Three hours later they would know what we knew—the Emmy had gotten away from me once again.

But you know what?

That's my luck.

Always has been.

You know what else?

I can't imagine what it would be like any other way.

I'M ACTUALLY GOOD AT THIS.

I've got it down to a science.

And, between you and me, it always makes for some pretty funny stories.

WHO WANTS TO BE ME?

Who Wants to Be A PETTY THIEF?

A nyway, here's what my sainted mother always liked to tell me whenever she thought I was in danger of getting too big for my britches—

"Hey, Mister Big Shot, the poorhouse is right around the corner!"

Mothers have a way of keeping things in perspective.

Of course, I've never forgotten her words.

And my little black cloud doesn't let me forget them, even if I wanted to. I've always had fun joking about living under this permanent little dark cloud that follows me around—keeping me in check, keeping me humble, keeping me . . .

FROM EVER EXPERIENCING A LIFE OF SIMPLICITY AND EASE!

Things just happen to me, all right? At times, it seems like everything happens to me. But, in truth, I'm a pretty lucky guy. I also just happen to be a lucky guy who lives his life under a little dark cloud—and can I tell you something?

I'M GETTING SICK OF IT!

It's never been easy being me. Some days are better than others, of course. For instance, there was the day I learned that I would become the host of a new little ABC prime-time quiz show called *Who Wants to Be a Millionaire.* That day couldn't have gone any better. Especially since I had to beat my brains in to even be considered for the job. Michael Davies—our young executive producer who discovered the program on British television—likes to say that my name was always on the short list.

Can I promise you something?

MY NAME WAS NEVER ON ANY SHORT LIST!

It wasn't even on a long list.

The big names in contention were Phil Donahue, Montel Williams, Maury Povich, and Bill Cullen—and Bill has been dead for several years! They were calling Bill over on the Other Side—*"Bill, where are you? We need you! Please, come back!"*

But they weren't calling Regis!

Regis had to fight for it.

Regis had to claw for it.

Regis almost had to kill for it.

Because I knew that this show would be a success—with or without me. But who could have known it would be as big a success as it was, and is? Who could have known when it debuted in August 1999 and aired on thirteen consecutive nights that it would dominate the ratings on each and every one of those nights like no show in recent memory? Who could have known it would change the landscape of prime-time network television and—

Wait a second . . .

I'll get back to that in a minute.

Before things get too carried away, I just want to make sure you believe me when I talk about my little dark cloud. Let me take you back to the night we taped our last *Millionaire* episode that August. Each one of those initial thirteen shows was taped on the night before it aired. So, by this time, we were part of a runaway sensation. Everywhere I went people would chase me down to say, "I want to be a millionaire!" And, of course, the inevitable—"Is that your final answer?" As the host of the show, I was suddenly the living embodiment of million-dollar madness.

Anyway, this was a Saturday night and, at that time, we had been doing all of our tapings at the Sony Music Studios facility at Fifty-third Street and Ninth Avenue. (We've since moved to the former studios of *Good Morning America* just around the corner from where I broadcast *Live!* each morning.) Our offices there were makeshift and I had been using a large upstairs room as my dressing area. That's where I would change out of my street clothes and climb into those spiffy dark suits before every taping. But we were temporary interlopers on the premises and lots of people would come and go during the course of an evening. Nobody ever bothered to even lock a door.

So that night, as usual, I got out of my casual clothes, laid them somewhere with my wallet and keys, put on the monochromatic *Millionaire* ensemble, and went downstairs to do the show. Afterward, I came back up, changed back into my clothes, collected my belongings, then got in a car that took me up to our weekend house in Connecticut. The next morning, I got up and went to church for Sunday mass. Then came the time of the tithing when the guy passes the collection basket down the pews on a long stick. So I reached for my wallet where I knew I had two hundred bucks. I don't usually carry that much money, but I had been to the bank the day before and hadn't touched it since. So I opened the wallet and—

It was empty!

Credit cards were there, but not a single dollar!

Not even a dime.

I had nothing.

Someone had crept into that dressing room during the taping and quietly slipped the two hundred bucks out of my wallet. And I didn't even have the chance to ask whoever took the money—*"Is that your final answer?!"*

But, meanwhile, here was the guy with the stick wiggling that basket in front of my nose!

He had that expectant stare.

Probably thinking, Let's see what Mr. Millionaire is going to drop in there.

Other parishioners were looking at me now, too, wondering what was taking me so long.

What was I supposed to do now?

Tell him I was robbed?

How could this happen to me?

All I could do was look him straight in the eye, clear my throat and mouth the words, "No. Not today."

All right, I felt like a cheap bum.

He probably thought, *This guy tries to give away millions of dollars every night and he doesn't have a dollar to give the church?!*

I was violated, then humiliated.

And it happened right there in church, yet.

My mother was right.

Sometimes that poorhouse can creep up on you in the strangest places.

SHE WANTED ME OUT OF THE HOUSE!

None of this could have happened to me if it wasn't for Joy.

(Nothing good ever really does.)

But in the case of *Millionaire,* it's especially true.

And the reason is very simple:

SHE COULDN'T STAND ME HANGING AROUND THE APARTMENT ALL AFTERNOON!

My work as the cohost of *Live!* basically ends each morning at ten o'clock. For years, I would then keep myself busy at the office until lunchtime. Then, every day, I would go off to a nearby restaurant with Gelman and Art Moore, our executive in charge of *Live!* The one whose job I've never understood. We would lunch.

Every single day.

For years.

And years.

The three of us.

Sitting at some table.

Staring at each other.

Chewing food.

We ran out of interesting conversation somewhere around 1991. But all we had was each other.

And it was *boring*.

God, it was boring.

After lunch, I would go home.

What woman wouldn't be thrilled to have her husband there with her all afternoon, day after day after day?

Exactly.

No woman alive would want that.

I GOT ON HER NERVES.

Even I began to question my life. I started wondering about the point of my own existence. I started feeling a little sorry for myself. I even talked about it on the air with Kathie Lee one day—

ME: What have I done with my life? I spent it in front of this stupid camera! For what?! It drives me crazy when I think of the way I squandered my life.

K.L.: The sad thing is, he really means that. You said that to me privately the other day and I got very upset.

ME: An unremarkable life!

5

K.L.: You're so wrong.

ME: Doing a little show in the morning?! Please! It means nothing in the grand scheme of things! Unremarkable! I've got a better word: insignificant! You think I'm kidding? I mean it from the bottom of my insignificant heart. I don't want to talk about it anymore.

K.L.: You need therapy.

ME: I came to the wrong place for it, I'll tell you that much!

Yes, that tragic display went out over national airwaves just two years ago. A man shouldn't be seen like that, I know.

The truth is I was coming home each day as Joy was leaving.

How much time could I spend at the gym?

I was bored.

She said I needed to do something to fill my afternoons.

JOY: Well, I just thought that we needed to have separate time. So I said, "You really need an afternoon job." I remember filling in for Kathie Lee one morning and discussing this on the air. I said that Regis needed, at the very least, a hobby to occupy himself in the afternoons. Viewers faxed in their suggestions of hobbies he could take up. One was that he could work in the garden with Mrs. Greenthumbs and call himself Mr. Greentoes. Another was that Regis could walk dogs for people in the neighborhood who work all day. And there was also the suggestion that he could hold my packages while I'm shopping.

That one really hurt.

But then, not too long afterward, I began hearing about this British quiz show that seemed bound for repackaging on American television. I got a tape of the show from my agent at William Morris, Jimmy Griffin, and I was knocked out. No show in history had ever offered a prize of a million dollars. And no show had as many other intriguing dramatic elements—the futuristic lighting, the pulsating music, the pressure of that win-or-lose moment with each new question, and the concept of those lifelines. There was an in-your-face human intimacy to it all that struck a familiar chord with me. There was something very personal about this show.

I've always liked to broadcast in a personal way.

I never knew any other way to do it!

And that's when I started banging down the door to get a shot at hosting this thing. I became a man possessed. They couldn't get rid of me. Yes . . .

I HAD TO BE THEIR FINAL ANSWER.

And, lo and behold, that's the way it worked out.

Just before the show debuted, I guested on David Letterman's *Late Show* and told David—tongue in cheek, but actually hoping it would happen—that I was going to save the ABC television network with this new show called *Who Wants to Be a Millionaire.* A few people in the audience gasped. A lot more of them laughed. It was such an audacious statement that people remembered it.

Two nights later, I went on CNN with Larry King, who asked me, "Why do you want to do this show?" And again I joked, "BECAUSE I AM HERE TO SAVE THE ABC TELEVISION NETWORK!" But Larry, being Larry, took me seriously. He said, "What do you mean?" I said, "Well, who's going to do it if I don't?" He said, "I don't know."

Larry, please, it was a joke!

But that's exactly what happened. Forget the odds, forget the jokes (for a minute, anyway). *Millionaire* took off like a rocket that August— which was the month, as the wise guys noted, when no one cares what's on TV. Anything decent looks good in August, they said. Just to make sure, ABC brought it back in November—right in the middle of those crucial ratings sweeps. It was even bigger in November. Bill Carter of *The*

New York Times called it a *national phenomenon*—and that's what it was. It was the biggest hit television had seen in a quarter century and, yes, it saved the network.

The following May, I found myself standing on a stage elevator two floors below the main stage at Radio City Music Hall—where I had lost so many Emmys over the years. The reason I was there was to make a special appearance at what they call "upfronts" in the TV business—the first official unveiling to media and advertisers of the network's fall season schedule. Down in that elevator, I could hear Stu Bloomberg, ABC's head programmer, begin to introduce me. Then the elevator began to move upward. There were laser lights, smoke, *2001* theme music, applause—and up I rose. Then I walked down the steps to my spot onstage to face six thousand people.

And I said, "All right, take a look at me, everybody! Here I am—the guy who saved the ABC television network! And I would have done it sooner. All they had to do was ask!"

But, to tell you the truth, nothing saved that network more than Joy asking me to get out of the house.

How do women know so much?

HERE'S MY FINAL ANSWER!

Can I tell you something?

I did not invent this phrase.

I had nothing to do with this phrase.

Like just about every other aspect of the *Millionaire* show—excluding me—it came over from Great Britain. The network lawyers insist that the contestants confirm that each answer is, indeed, the final answer—otherwise they could come back and say, "You know, I was going to pick something else, but I rushed it." So we have to ask that question in no uncertain terms. Even so, the British host, or presenter—Chris Tarrant—

had told me to beware. He said people came up to him constantly and, for a laugh, repeated the phrase to his face . . .

"IS THAT YOUR FINAL ANSWER?"

I had no idea how true this would be.

On the street, the only thing I ever heard for years was—*"Where's Kathie Lee?"* People thought that was a scream. People thought I would think that was a scream. I would say, "She's at home singing Cassidy a new lullaby! What did I ever do to you?"

But, suddenly, that all changed.

Suddenly, I would quietly walk down the street and every other person was asking me if that was my final answer.

I hadn't spoken a word when they spotted me—but they wondered if I had given my final answer.

MY FINAL ANSWER TO WHAT???????

All right, it's been flattering. It proves that the show has touched a nerve in all of us. Nothing could, or does, make me happier than that. But still . . .

Please!!!

What am I supposed to say?

It gets a little weird.

Some people actually think they're saying this to me as though I haven't heard it before.

I've heard it before.

Not that I mind, really.

But even Larry King wrote in his regular Monday *USA Today* column—under the heading of "Unsolicited Advice for the Producers of *Who Wants to Be a Millionaire*"—that I no longer should have to ask, "Is that your final answer?" Larry wrote: "Reege looks uncomfortable doing it, we feel uncomfortable watching it."

God forbid that Larry King be uncomfortable!

He should try walking down the street with me.

But, then again, Larry also wrote in that column: "Never, ever, let

Regis Philbin go. He's a national treasure and an essential part of your program."

You know, I always thought Larry King was a very smart guy.

I've always said, "IF LARRY SAYS IT, THEN IT'S GOOD ENOUGH FOR ME!"

But, just to keep him happy, next time you see us on the street together, ask me to phone a friend, instead.

I'm sure Larry will happily cover the charges.

TAKE MY LOOK, PLEASE!!

All of a sudden, I'm a fashion icon.

Forty years in front of a television camera and suddenly what I'm wearing is important. Who knew? Of course, it only happened because of the *Millionaire* show. When I went to London last year with Michael Davies, our executive producer, I noticed that the British host, Chris Tarrant, was wearing dark conservative tones. **Everything was dark.** Suit, shirt, tie—all but his yellow thatch of hair. And since we were going to re-create every aspect of the British version of the show, I knew that would become my wardrobe as well. Davies and Vincent Rubino, the supervising producer, went to the Beau Brummel store in SoHo, which had dressed me for ten years on *Live!*, and selected my new suits—all dark blue and black and gray with matching solid-colored ties and shirts. Of course, solid ties and shirts have been around for a long time, but when I began wearing them on those thirteen straight nights of prime-time TV in August 1999, the reaction was instantaneous and very surprising.

Forty years in television—nobody noticed or cared what I wore! But now I was a walking fashion statement, a stylemaker, a Seventh Avenue trendsetter.

(Hey, I just wore what they told me to!)

Suddenly, it seemed like everyone in the apparel industry was calling my agent, Jimmy Griffin at William Morris, about a Regis line of something . . . of anything—even socks and underwear. At first we resisted, but then by the following spring, the requests became overwhelming. So we went with Phillips-Van Heusen for a line of solid-colored shirts and ties. It was to be called **The Regis Collection**—a name that still makes me wince. The Regis Collection! My God, what would my boyhood pal from the Bronx, Freakin' Finelli, think?

But even before we began speaking about the idea with Mark Weber, the Van Heusen president, solid shirts and ties were already selling like hotcakes in men's stores around the country. Haberdashers had started calling it "The *Millionaire* look." It was *Millionaire* this, *Millionaire* that— all anybody had to do to sell a shirt was to throw around the name *Millionaire*. What exactly had we started here?!

Finally, just before Father's Day, we launched The (*I'm wincing again!*) Regis Collection at Macy's on Thirty-fourth Street in New York. The store dressed six windows with blown-up photographs of me—from childhood pictures and onward. A high school marching band lined my pathway through the store. Mobs of paparazzi were clicking away with their cameras. TV crews were chasing me around the aisles and filming everything. It was very exciting and somewhat surreal . . .

And all because Regis wears solid colors!!

That was supposed to be the only appearance I was to make in conjunction with the clothing line, due to my extremely tight taping schedule with both shows. But, you know, that's never the case. Requests always keep coming and, the next thing we knew, Jimmy had heard from the Men's Neckwear Association, whose members wanted to present me with an award for "*reinvigorating*" men's ties! (Is that what I did? Reinvigorate ties??) Frankly, I couldn't believe my eyes when I read this quote from some revered style guru in *The New York Times*: "We call it the Philbinization of neckwear." WHAT EXACTLY DOES THAT *MEAN*?

Well, one thing it meant was that the tie guys wanted to give me an award. It would only take fifteen minutes. "You're in, you're out—easy," Jimmy assured me. And so you say yes and one day that luncheon date is upon you. So the day arrived and I left my offices at WABC around twelve-thirty. If I'm there at one, I'm out at one-fifteen. I can do that.

Five minutes into the ride en route to the Roosevelt Hotel located at Forty-fifth and Madison, my town car is rear-ended at Fifty-fifth and Seventh Avenue. Just great. The driver pulls over, gets out—and that's the last I see of him! So it's taxi time, but it's also lunchtime—meaning no available cabs in sight. Now it's getting late and I don't want to keep the tie people waiting, so I get out into the street on Seventh Avenue to flag down anything moving. Pedestrians are getting quite a show.

"Hey, Mr. Millionaire, where's your limo?!"

"HERE'S YOUR LIMO!" I want to answer back, but instead I smile. No cabs anywhere. Not one.

Now people are shouting, *"Is this gonna be your final ride?"*

"HERE'S YOUR FINAL RIDE!" I want to say, but I just keep smiling.

I go on thinking very hopefully: *Remember—this is just fifteen minutes. You're in, you're out.*

Meanwhile, I can't even get in a cab!

Finally, I see one with no passengers. I jump in and am on my way. The cabbie is wearing a turban and I think of all the Letterman jokes about cabbies who wear turbans. But I'm thankful I've got him. The traffic across town is murder, of course. Already it's been forty-five minutes since I set out for this event and now I'm just arriving.

The banquet room is arranged so that you must walk through the entire room to get to the head table. *Which means everybody sees me show up late.* I sit down and notice that Mike Jarvis, the basketball coach at St. John's, is among the awardees. Amid a flurry of autograph-seeking neckwear enthusiasts, a man aproaches me and says he will introduce me and present the award. I usually tell emcees to please keep it short—just mention *Live! With Regis & Kathie Lee* and *Who Wants to Be a*

Millionaire—no need for more. But I'm distracted by the picture-taking and autograph-signing and don't manage to get this across to him. So he steps to the podium and begins his welcoming remarks.

And, right away, I distinctly hear him say "Regis Philbin." But I'm still a little discombobulated from the accident and the rush to get here and all the attention around me. I realize—*Great, I'm up already*. I walk briskly to the podium where the emcee suddenly waves me off. That's when I found out that he didn't actually introduce me. *He just mentioned my name!* But it's too late—I'm up there next to him, feeling a little silly.

And inside I'm screaming:

So let me accept the award! Let me say thanks and get off and get back to the studio where another Millionaire *show waits to be taped! Please, Tie-Man, please . . .*

But no.

This guy *wants to introduce me!* And I mean *really introduce me*—by reading every single word of a five-page biography that is badly in need of a rewrite and an update. Nothing makes me more uncomfortable than long glowing introductions at these kinds of events. **It's just a tie award, for God's sake.** Let me accept it graciously and say good-bye!

But now he's into it—*yes, it was back in San Diego in the early sixties when young Regis Philbin had a dream . . .*

And there I am standing next to this guy wanting to die!

I tried to interrupt him.

But he read it all—every word, every page.

. . . The long journey to Hollywood, the ups, the downs, the Joey Bishop Show, *the first morning show,* AM Los Angeles *in the seventies, the silly movies in which I made cameo appearances like* Death Flight 577 *on ABC (which mostly just died in the ratings), the Cable Health Network show, a commercial I made for Burger King, Mae West's last movie . . . and on to New York and* The Morning Show *and* Live! *with Kathie Lee . . . and on and on . . . AND ON!!*

And I'm still right there beside him, looking and feeling like a dork.

Finally he winds it up and declares me the Duke of Dark Tones and the Sultan of Satin—*all right* already!—and he hands me the award. And I realize that I haven't prepared a speech. Nothing. Now what? I look at my award—a very nice piece of cut glass with a striped tie etched on it. (*Striped* tie?) And I say, "You know, I never thought I'd get an award for my tie before I got one for my TV show!"

JUST BECAUSE I DRESS LIKE ONE . . .

By the way, let me tell you about something very t-y-p-i-c-a-l that happened to this so-called Sultan of Satin just a couple of months before that. Phillips-Van Heusen decided that there should be a properly swanky unveiling of (*ahhh, here we go again*) The Regis Collection for the media. This would be the big announcement. An event to be covered by international press and, more importantly, by *Entertainment Tonight*! Can you get any hotter? Anyway, the honchos decided where better to project this exciting image than in the private upstairs room at New York's famous '21' Club, where millionaires flock to dine—because only they can afford it!

So there we all gathered at noon surrounded by lots of media types, lots of top Van Heusen people, plus me and Jimmy ("You're in, you're out") Griffin. We did our unveiling. I told everyone how weird it felt to have a Collection named after me. It was a quite unusual experience, but we had fun with it. Afterward, a half-dozen of the big Van Heusen bosses—all very enthused—asked Jimmy and me to go downstairs for a little celebratory lunch in the clubby main-floor bar room. I told them I couldn't stay long because I had to run off to tape another *Millionaire* show. But they convinced us to come down for a quick bite and a toast to the new enterprise. And they were still toasting and laughing when Jimmy and I had to excuse ourselves to get back to work. I thanked them for everything—including the great lunch—and then I was gone.

Eventually, I guess, the Van Heusen guys each had to slip back to work, too. And I guess—what with all the excitement of the day—somebody forgot to pay the lunch tab.

At '21'.

And I guess the staff at '21' didn't know what to do with the bill.

But they did recognize *one guy* who sat at that table.

All I know is that a few weeks later the awful truth arrived in my office mail. Celebratory lunch: $771.93.

Thanks, guys. Now go sell some shirts.

'21' Club Inc.
21 West 52nd Street
New York, NY 10019
212/582 7200

21

Statement

Please return stub
with remittance

PAGE 1 OF 1

To
Mr. Regis Philbin
WABC-TV
7 Lincoln Square
New York, NY 10023

026328   026328

STATEMENT DATE   05/31/00

Date	Reference	Charges	Credits	Balance
050200	Bar Room Lunch CK 1368	771.93		771.93
	Please pay this amount >	771.93		771.93

To avoid late charges, payment must be received by 06/30/00.
For your next important family event... whether its 21st
birthday, a graduation or an engagement party,
please consider having your celebration at "21".

Thank you for your
prompt payment

GIVE ME A PIECE OF TREBEK!

Okay, here's what I think:

First of all, *Jeopardy!* host Alex Trebek is great at what he does, one of the best in the business. He's been around a long time and he runs a very classy, successful show. But his show doesn't air in prime time. Which means he has never been number one in prime time. And, also, it means that *he never saved a network in his life!* So let's be frank, here:

HE'S JEALOUS OF ME!

Meanwhile, Trebek thinks he's Einstein. He spouted off to the press about how easy our *Millionaire* questions are. He said our contestants get stumped by questions like "What's the usual color of Post-its?"

Come on, Alex, get over it!

We'll put *you* in the hot seat and see if *you* can remember what color Post-its are! That's right, I'd like to strap him in the chair for Celebrity *Millionaire* and see what Mr. Big Shot with all his fancy French pronunciations *really* knows!

In all seriousness, I think Alex was just giving us a little good-natured teasing. He and I have been rivaling it out for quite a while, ever since I made a fool of myself on Celebrity *Jeopardy!* Twice, yet! Which is why it's his turn to come on our show!

Both times they asked me to be on *Jeopardy!*, I bravely agreed: "Whatever you want, Alex. I'm there." The first time I did it, they stuck me at the third podium and the stupid buzzer wouldn't work! I whined about that for years. I annoyed those *Jeopardy!* people to death! They were indignant. They said, "Nobody else ever complained."

But me, I complain!

That didn't stop me from going back and doing the show again a few years later. This time they put me at the first podium just to shut me up. *But that buzzer didn't work, either!* No wonder Alex was smiling up there. And you know who else was smiling? A couple of technicians who drifted behind me.

I SWEAR I SAW THEM CUT SOME WIRES!

I'm not casting aspersions here, I'm just telling you what I *think* I saw. In any case, not a *peep* came from that buzzer. That's twice in a row! Honestly, I believe that there's *some kind of conspiracy against me!* I'm sure of it!

And I had really studied and practiced that time. For days, everything that came out of my mouth was in the form of a question! Backstage before we taped, just to be safe, I practiced some more with Stephen King, who was also a contestant—and I knew *every one of the questions!*

Boom, boom, boom!

I knew the capitals of every state in the union—cold! Didn't matter. *Not once* did Alex ask for the capital of Montana. Instead he had all those weird categories: French Writers? Scottish Kings? What do I know about French writers and Scottish kings? Give me something *I know!* Like Italian cooking. *I know* my spaghetti and meatballs! Please!

And to be honest, when I got out there under the lights, behind my little podium, I froze. It didn't really scare me. I just couldn't get the brain-to-hand coordination you need for that show.

Needless to say, I didn't do so hot.

In fact, it was ABSOLUTELY HUMILIATING!

So let it be known: I'm ready for a *Jeopardy!* rematch.

But this time, no fancy lights, no buzzers, no audience—just me and Trebek, mano a mano, duking it out! If he won't come on *Millionaire*, we'll see how well he does on his own show without the answers in front of him!

Incidentally, what *is* the usual color of Post-its?

THEN SAJAK TRIED
TO DRIVE ME NUTS

I've always suspected that Pat Sajak wants to be me. I mean, how would *you* like to do *Wheel of Fortune* every day? Furthermore, we've seen him host his own late night talk show. We've seen him jump in to pinch-hit for me and survive a week with Kathie Lee. You can see that he wants more of what I have. But let me tell you, Saj, beware of what you wish for! It ain't easy, all right?

Anyway, he came on *Live!* one morning not long after *Millionaire* pandemonium first broke and he slowly, intrepidly, calculatedly tried to beat my brains out! What is it with these guys?

ME: So, have you heard I have a little quiz show?

P.S.: No, have you mentioned it on the air yet?

ME: Any advice from the old Saj one?

P.S.: How long does it take to tape a show?

ME: An hour show takes about two hours, sometimes longer.

P.S.: You must be screwing up a lot. We do a half-hour show in a half hour.

ME: Oh, do you *really*?

P.S.: Why does it take two hours?

ME: Let me ask you something. What is the prize for this *Wheel* thing? What does the contestant who wins get? CAN THEY WIN A MILLION DOLLARS?

P.S.: How many have won a million?

ME: None so far. And what kind of a STUPID question was THAT!?!

P.S.: So, theoretically, they could win a million.

ME: I had a half-million dollar winner once. What's the biggest prize you ever gave away?

P.S.: Somewhere in the $150,000 range.

ME: Please! . . . But I like the game show work. I think what we do on a talk show is a little more difficult than that.

P.S.: No, I've done this, too. I know it's not all that difficult, Regis.

ME: Whoa, whoa! It's difficult to get a rating! How long did that show last anyway?

P.S.: We ran about a year and a half, which is not a bad run.

ME: But it's not fifteen, sixteen, FORTY-ONE YEARS, IS IT?

P.S.: No, that's why I didn't give up my day job.

ME: And that day job takes up how many days a year?

P.S.: Here comes the bitterness again. We do five shows in a day. We do thirty-nine days a year. But I don't have the fire in the belly. Difficult to have a full-time job again.

ME: Aw, isn't that too bad. Don't want to ever have a full-time job again. I WANT TO WORK THIRTY-NINE DAYS A YEAR!

K.L.: I sense a lot of sexual tension between the two of you.

SAM DONALDSON BELONGS ON HIS KNEES!

People magazine invited Joy and my son, Dan, and me to sit at its table at the last annual President's Correspondents Dinner in Washington, DC. That spring night, the Hilton Ballroom was crawling with three thousand journalists who had come to hear the President do stand-up comedy material and get even with all of them. And since this was President Clinton's final hurrah at this dinner, he pulled out all the stops—even starred in a hysterical little movie about his last days in the White House—and made himself a very tough act for emcee Jay Leno to follow. But being trapped in this jam-packed room with all these media big shots really drove something home for me—

There is nothing like the power of prime-time television.

Kathie Lee and I killed ourselves every morning for fifteen years—and what did it mean?

NOTHING.

I had been doing daytime and late-night television for forty years total—and what did it mean?

NOTHING.

But the crushing popularity of the *Millionaire* show has changed all that. All of a sudden, I'm the overnight success story who came from nowhere! All of a sudden, these jaded correspondents are climbing all over me! They want pictures taken. They want autographs. They want me to judge their ties. And, more than anything else, they want me to never find our table! I swear to God—it took the Secret Service to get us to our seats.

I HAVE NEVER NEEDED THE SECRET SERVICE BEFORE IN MY LIFE!

And let me tell you something:

I LIKED IT!

Anyway, before we went down to Washington, Gelman had warned me that Sam Donaldson and Cokie Roberts wanted me to do their Sunday morning ABC news program, *This Week.* Now, the last thing you want to do on a whirlwind weekend is to get up and go on any kind of show—but maybe especially that one. What am I supposed to do—go toe-to-toe with George Will and George Stephanopoulos? So I declined. But now, in this ballroom, I'm dead meat. They sent a producer over to find me. Joy said, "Don't do it." I said, "I'll try not to." But then Sam and Cokie themselves hunt me down. Sam starts yelling and screaming and telling me we'll have fun with it and, frankly, I'm helpless. You can't say no to Sam Donaldson! So, finally, I said, "Okay, I'll be there. Just get away from me, for crying out loud!"

Where was my Secret Service when I *really* needed it?

The next morning, I get up early and go over to ABC Studios in Washington. Senators are all over the place, nothing but senators everywhere you look. There's Max Cleland, who lost his legs and one arm in Vietnam, and is now a senator in Georgia. There's Senator Hagel from Nebraska. And others, too. Preceding my segment is a long, intense discussion between George Will, George Stephanopoulos, Sam and Cokie about whether gays should be allowed in the Boy Scouts.

ABOUT THIS TIME, I'M LOOKING AROUND FOR AN EXIT!

What have I got to say about this?

I had nothing to say!

But after a commercial break, they came back to talk about the Correspondents Dinner last night. So out steps Regis for his special commentary. There I am with Sam and Cokie and I'm giving the President a detailed terrific review of his performance. And then Sam pulls out a ten-dollar bill. He says, "Now, in the parlance of your show, let's ask you the $64,000 question." I said, "Sam, what's the *matter* with you? *The $64,000 Question* went out thirty-five years ago! The name of the show is *Who Wants to Be a Millionaire,* and nowadays we have a million-dollar question—and you ought to get down on your knees and thank God for that show or you wouldn't be sitting here right now! You'd be doing this show on a park bench if it wasn't for that show!"

I let him have it.

For once, Sam Donaldson was speechless!

"Where's Kathie LEE?"

Oh, Kathie Lee.
Where to begin, where to begin . . .

Well, I guess I should begin at the end.

. . . And she lives happily ever after.

And she will, you know. Kathie Lee has become an industry unto herself. Clothing line, cosmetics, cruises, songwriting, CDs—it's amazing. Years ago, I saw her dictating to her assistant one day and I realized what a mogul she'd become. And that's also when I understood that our show was PLAYTIME for her! It was the one hour of her day when she wasn't making executive decisions! On *Live!*, she didn't have to conquer the world—so she conquered me instead. Or, at least, tried her best to.

Anyway, after a decade and a half of putting up with me, she felt it was time to spread her wings, to soar like an eagle! And I think I know what made her do it—Broadway. The Great White Way. After all these years, it finally got to her. She's been onstage her whole life. But once you've done Broadway, there's no turning back. There's a huge gap between big-time theater and guerrilla television.

And that's exactly what *Live!* is, what it was from the get-go—

Guerrilla television.

You say what you think, you lay it on the line and it's out there, baby! No retakes, no edits, no regrets! Okay, *some* regrets, but not big ones. And fifteen years really is a long time for two people to stay together in that kind of racket.

And now she's gone.

And to be honest, I kind of miss her.

More than kind of, really.

She came to me fifteen years ago with cute little bangs and a MAJOR ATTITUDE. I took her under my wing, molded her into the refined, demure superstar she is today. I remember the first day we worked together in 1985. She ran up Sixty-seventh Street from *Good Morning America*, where she'd been pinch-hitting for Joan Lunden. She raced into our studio wearing her running shoes, flushed and panting, and that's how we began our cohosting relationship. "My new cohost can't even get here on time!" I teased her. And that's how it all began.

You want the truth about her?

Here it is, plain and simple: Kathie Lee Gifford is an irrepressible, indefatigable, unsinkable, ambitious whirlwind. I'm only one man, but she's definitely more than one woman, and she would have made it big-time wherever she worked.

With Kathie, there was always an edge. We wanted that edge. We didn't mind needling one another, whether gently or mercilessly, to get it. We knew what we had to do to grab that audience and make them pay attention—then make them come back the next day and the day after that.

Somehow, it worked.

We clicked.

Our producer, Gelman, who thinks he knows everything, says the subliminal reason for our success together was sexual tension. I keep telling him he's nuts. There was no sexual tension. At least, not on my part. When I think it over, though, I realize that maybe once in a while she wondered about it.

But probably not.

Incidentally, have I told you about the time Kathie and I slept together? It's one of my favorite stories . . .

Boy, was it hot.

And steamy.

The weather, I mean.

Providence, Rhode Island, gets pretty sweltering in July. We were down there performing at the Warwick Theater toward the end of one of our summer concert tours. For this particular engagement, we had to share a mobile home dressing room. Kitchen, living room, two dressing areas and a bathroom in between. The afternoon rehearsal was short, so we had a couple of hours to kill before getting dressed. This was the first time we'd ever been all alone together before a show.

So Kathie put on her robe and curled up on one of the couches in the living room. I got comfortable on my couch. And we both watched television without saying a word. After a while, we both dozed off, me on my couch, she on hers. Which I guess technically means that we slept together.

Disappointed?

GET OVER IT!

The point is there's more sexual tension between me and my urologist than there was between me and Kathie Lee!

So much for Gelman and his theories.

SOMEHOW I SURVIVED!

In truth, Kathie Lee was always supportive and encouraging when I started hosting *Who Wants to Be a Millionaire*. I think I was more surprised by the show's success than she was. All right, she didn't initially like my new prime-time wardrobe. Too dark, she said. She liked me better in lighter shades—to go along with my happy carefree demeanor that she knew so well from our mornings together WHEN I WAS FIGHTING FOR MY LIFE SITTING NEXT TO HER!

Anyway, David Letterman and his writers had some fun imagining her reaction to my good luck, which prompted this Top Ten List when *Millionaire* returned after its initial summer run:

From the Home Office in Wahoo, Nebraska, it's the Top Ten List:

TOP TEN SIGNS KATHIE LEE IS TRYING TO KILL REGIS

10. She carved into his office door: "Who wants to be a corpse?"
9. Traces of cyanide found in his twenty-six morning cups of coffee.
8. While air-kissing Regis, she stabs him with her over-sprayed hair.
7. Asks him, "Is your estate in order? Are you sure? Final answer?"
6. Tells husband Frank that Regis satisfies her like no man she's ever been with.
5. He keeps finding legs of his stool half sawed through.
4. Wired to Regis' car—A bomb made completely from Max Factor makeup.
3. During cooking segment, she "accidentally" held his head in deep-fat fryer for an hour.
2. Regis trapped in elevator while her Christmas CD plays again and again.
1. Cody found wandering studio chanting: "Must kill Regis."

MY FATHER, GELMAN

And what about Gelman? Seeing as there's almost thirty years between us, he should be like a son to me. But he's not. Most of the time I feel like he's my father. Most every weekday morning from nine to ten, you'll see him hovering paternally in the wings, making sure we're on time and on target. God, how he *hovers!*

I HATE IT WHEN HE HOVERS!

Like a mother hen looking over her brood!

But thank God he's there. I need somebody to blame when I'm on the air. And I can blame Gelman for everything. In fact, I *do* blame him for everything. Everyone ought to have a Gelman.

He started as an intern on my local WABC *Morning Show.* I don't even remember seeing him back then. He was a small blip on the show's radar. But eventually, he rose in the ranks to become our executive producer, top dog. You wanna be on the show, you gotta go through Gelman. And Gelman's a very strong Leo—and so was Kathie Lee! But, believe me, he's no pushover. He may *look* like a pushover, but he's tough. What do you expect? I raised him from a pup! Then I put him on the screen and now he may be one of the best-known executive producers on television.

For years I would kid Gelman about his die-hard bachelor attitude and lifestyle: "It's time to think about the future, Gelman. The cottage, the white picket fence, the little Gelmans!" So around 1994, he took a step in the right direction. He met a girl named Laurie Hibberd, now an entertainment reporter for *The Early Show* on CBS. Gelman first met her when he accompanied me to an interview for the Miami, Florida, Fox station where she worked at the time. She spent the obligatory four minutes with me, then asked, "Do you mind if I do a minute or two with Gelman?" This was at the height of Gelman-mania—and I was just about done molding him into a huge star. So they sat down in the living room of my hotel suite and began the interview. But after a few minutes, the words began to stumble, their eyes locked and they just sat there looking at each other! "You kids want to be alone?" I got so embarrassed, I LEFT THE ROOM! MY OWN ROOM! And that's how it all began.

Now, finally, six and a half years later, they're Mr. and Mrs. Michael Gelman. They would have tied the knot sooner, but Gelman wasn't through raising me yet! Anyhow, they got married in a beautiful ceremony at an estate in the Hamptons. I was one of the groomsmen.

Not the best man, mind you—just a groomsman.

"What do the groomsmen do?" I asked him.

"They escort people to their seats."

"I'm a big TV star! How did I wind up being an usher?!"

I was dissed! I got the Gelman Dis! That's the thanks I got for making him who he is today!

It's all right, though, I can handle it.

Aside from that, everything went flawlessly; it was definitely a first-class affair. Of course. It's Gelman producing for himself. He would have nothing less. I've never seen Gelman lay out such big bucks! Even the Porta Potti's scattered around the property were like mini luxury condos!

Like I said, Gelman decides what we'll do every weekday morning. And that includes wacky stunts that might kill, maim and/or humiliate me. But what does Gelman care? It's not *his* life and career he's risking! As long as this stuff brings in the almighty ratings, he's satisfied. And, when it comes to ratings, we'll try anything. Well, *almost* anything. I put my foot down when Gelman suggested I run with the bulls in Pamplona. But I've boxed and wrestled and hang-glided and put my life on the line. I've taken on eight-year-old girls in piano competitions. And LOST! I've played eighty-year-old women in tennis. And LOST! I've worked undercover doling out french fries at McDonald's. I've grappled in the mud with a bikini-clad woman who wanted my blood. And you know what? If this is what entertains our audience, it's worth every minute of the excruciating pain and humiliation I'm forced to endure.

But, let me tell you something—one of these days, I'm gonna die in the line of duty. I know it.

Then who'll carry ABC on his shoulders?

East Side, West Side—Just Give Me CONVENIENCE!

You want one of those seamy confessions?

Here goes:

I watched the construction of the towering high-rise building we now live in . . . *with lust and longing in my heart!* It started going up in the mid-nineties at the corner of Sixty-Seventh and Columbus—directly across the street from our WABC studios where we do *Live!* Every day for a whole year, I studied the progress of the project and coveted everything about it. I said to myself, *This is exactly where I belong!* I knew that it would be so convenient to live there and just tiptoe across the street to work every morning. A two-minute commute! What could be better?

But since returning to New York from California, we had lived on the East Side where the girls went to school. And the East Side is terrific, believe me—unless, of course, you have to get a cab every morning and fight traffic and navigate your way across town through Central Park in order to get to the West Side where you and your cohost take on each other and all of America on a program broadcast live at nine o'clock. I constantly nudged Joy about the possibility of moving to the new building—there would be a Reebok gym and health club right on the premises as well as multiplex movie theaters and a covey of good restaurants around the corner!—but she wouldn't hear of it. She loved the East Side and that's where she wanted to stay. We had made a nice life in our Park Avenue apartment and I could see why she was hesitant to uproot herself. Plus, I guess there were some unforgettable memories attached to that place . . .

CAN'T A GUY GET A LITTLE SUN?

A STORY FROM J.J. PHILBIN:

When I was in eighth grade, we lived on the Upper East Side of Manhattan in a second-floor apartment overlooking Park Avenue.

I'll never forget one spring day when Joanna and I were sitting in the living room. I just happened to look out the window and saw the weirdest thing. "Oh, my God, Joanna! Check this out!" On the beautifully landscaped island that runs down the middle of Park Avenue, there was some bare-chested guy plopped in a lawn chair sunning himself on the lawn there among the tulips and shrubbery. He was wearing dark sunglasses and had a bunch of magazines piled next to him in the grass. Just basking in the rays like he was at the beach, totally oblivious to the whizzing traffic, gawking pedestrians and snooty neighborhood in general. So we called to our mom: "Mom, you have to look at this! Some guy is sunbathing on the Park Avenue island!"

She took one look and turned pale: "Oh, my God! That's your father!" *So she threw open the window and yelled:* **"Regis! Please come in here right now!"**

He came back up to the apartment muttering, had no idea what the problem was. "I wanted to get some sun! So what?"

We'd only been living in New York for a few years, so he was still used to his California comfort zone and didn't want to give it up. Honestly, it was sort of heartbreaking. And while he's much more settled now than he was then,

California must still be in his blood. Because to this day, if it's a day off and he sees a sunny patch of grass—doesn't matter where, really—he will take off his shirt, lay it on the ground and stretch out on it. But that's my dad. No excuses.

CAN'T A GUY HAVE A LITTLE FUN? (No, probably not, okay?)

A STORY FROM JOANNA PHILBIN:

Here's a Halloween story that happened right around the same time—J.J. and I must have been in seventh and eighth grades, like ages twelve and thirteen. Our building had tons of kids. So Halloween was always kind of a big deal—or as much as it can be in New York. The kids in the building were jumping on and off the elevator, hitting every apartment on every floor. So for about six hours, the doorbell just rang constantly, beginning around five o' clock.

You'd race to the door and give them candy, check out their costumes and wait for the next one. J.J. and I did most of the doling out. But, because we had homework to do, my dad took over the job after a few hours. And he was getting a little antsy and bored with the whole thing. Okay, he was annoyed! And he wanted to liven things up for himself. So somewhere in our house he found this really amazing and elaborate Freddy Krueger rubber mask. He probably brought it home from the show—but it was pretty horrifying and realistic. Scars, pockmarked cheeks—very gross.

He decided to put it on—"Okay, I'm going to have a little fun with this!"—and wait for the next trick-or-treater doorbell so he could lunge out into the hallway and give them a little performance. The next time the doorbell rang, there stood the eight-year-old son of the president of the co-op board. He was kind of a shy, fragile kid. And he was there just with his mother. This kid took one look at Dad and literally jumped in the air. He started climbing the walls! They had to like peel him off the ceiling and put him back in the elevator!

From what we could figure, the kid didn't speak to us again for years. We would see him in the mornings down in the lobby waiting to go to school and, every morning, he'd dart into the corner and cower from anyone in our family. My dad tried and tried to explain that it was only a little Halloween joke and told the parents how sorry he was. The parents understood but, for years, that little boy was traumatized whenever he saw my father. It's amazing that we weren't evicted from the building. The poor kid. Probably set him back about five years. But that's my dad's luck. A horrible but true story.

ANYWAY . . .

There was a week in the mid-nineties when Joy was cohosting with me on *Live!* And one morning she got a taste of what I'd been complaining about for years—that traffic-snarled trip across town. It's usually okay until you hit West Sixty-seventh Street. Then it's pure torture as you inch up that final block to the station.

This particular day, it was as horrendous as ever: limos side-by-side outside *Good Morning America,* a sanitation truck outside the Café des Artistes, plus a school bus and an oil truck, all sitting stationary, all immovable. And behind all of this, Joy and I sat trapped. I got such a kick out of her reaction. The Furies began to build in her and then came the eruption. She had a fit and this was only her second day on the job this week. I told her to try it for eleven years. That didn't help.

Not immediately anyway. So I continued to beg and plead with her to consider living in the building across the street from the studios. I'd say, "Wouldn't it be easier to live across the street, jump into ABC, do the show, and hop home for lunch?" She told me that's exactly why we weren't going to live across the street: "I don't want you coming home for lunch," she said. **"I married you for better or for worse, but not for lunch!"**

Then, one day in 1996, she finally gave in.

I couldn't believe it, but I wasn't going to question it, either. So we revisited the new building and looked around this terrific apartment more than fifty floors up that I'd shown her before. Even its beautiful panoramic views of the city had failed to sell her on the place during previous visits. But mysteriously, she'd changed her mind. Moving to the West Side might make for a new beginning, she said. And a new nest wouldn't feel as much like an empty nest with the girls gone at college. So we agreed to put in a bid.

"But if we get it," she warned me, "you're still not allowed to come home for lunch."

Well, we got it and we love it. As for lunch, I hardly ever go home anyway. For years I was stuck having lunch nearly every single day with Art Moore and Gelman. What a summit that was. It got to be a weight around my neck. But now because of the heavy schedule of *Millionaire* tapings—which, conveniently enough, we now do in the old *Good Morning America* studios down the block—our lunches are pretty much a thing of the past, and just in time too.

DON'T FOG
ME IN!

Once we got settled and Joy had finished decorating the place, we decided to throw a big Christmas cocktail party. So we invited some friends up to mix and mingle and take in our panoramic view of the city. The only thing I'd ever wanted before I check out of this life was a knockout view. And now I finally had one, so I wanted to share it with people! We're above the fiftieth floor and it's quite a spectacle to gaze out and see the billions of twinkling New York City lights and Central Park below and the vistas beyond the rivers.

Anyway, Joy put together a pretty impressive guest list for the party and, that night, there they all were: Kathie Lee and Frank, Barbara

Walters, Diane Sawyer and Mike Nichols, Chuck and Alyssa Grodin, Tony Bennett, Bryant and June Gumbel, Ron Silver, Jerry Orbach, even Gelman and Laurie—hey, it was the hottest! Let me tell you—Donald Trump was actually working the door like our greeter. And he doesn't even like shaking hands with people!

But there was one big problem.

It had been one of those overcast, gloomy days and, by nightfall, fog had rolled in.

Not just a little fog, either.

No, this turned out to be the WORST FOG-BOUND NIGHT I HAD EVER SEEN SINCE WE MOVED!

I thought somebody had scaled the side of the building and painted the windows with whitewash.

That's how thick the fog was.

I couldn't believe it.

And do you want to know something—I'm not just telling this to enhance the story—but after everybody left, *the fog lifted!*

Why *then?*

Why not an hour before, when everyone was still there, eating and drinking and laughing it up?!

I'll tell you why:

Because it's me.

That's the only logical reason I can think of.

THE BATHROOM DIALOGUE

JOY: I think when you get older, the most important thing in your life is privacy. Everyone should have a little privacy, if one can have that. Now we were fortunate enough to make sure when we got this apartment that we would each have our own bathroom.

That's right.

JOY: But Regis, for some reason or another, likes my bathtub. He comes in every night, brings his towel and—

Excuse me. In the distribution of bathrooms, Regis didn't wind up with a bathtub. NO BATHTUB FOR REGIS! So once in a while I sneak into her bathroom. Big deal.

JOY: Yes, but the last straw was when you slammed your shower door shut in a—I don't know, maybe you were having a little temper tantrum? But now you can't open it. So every morning he marches into my bathroom and now he's showering in there, too. And I resent that.

Well, once in a while the Bad Joy rises up from within . . .

JOY: I don't want to hear this.

And the Bad Joy can aggravate me. And, a few days earlier, suddenly the Bad Joy appeared and said something to really annoy me. So the shower door was open and I just gave it a little shot. That's all.

JOY: And now you can't open it.

There are two glass doors, right? One door stays firm and the other door opens and closes. So I pushed this door *rather vigorously* and the door went beyond the other door and is now locked in place behind it. But now I'm afraid to pull it because I might break the glass.

JOY: I think we get the idea. So what are you gonna do about this?

I'm gonna wait for the handyman to come. I'm not handy, you know.

JOY: Really? I had no idea.

MISSION: IMPOSSIBLE
RENTING A VIDEO

A few months after we moved to the West Side, Joy and I decided to rent a movie for the very first time at the Tower Video store across the street. Everything in our neighborhood is just steps away, which is supposed to make life a breeze.

But let me tell you—renting this video wasn't any breeze.

Okay, mostly it was my fault.

I walked out of the house without a wallet. But I hate to carry my wallet. It's a big bulky thing stuffed with cards and notes people give me. Very uncomfortable to sit on. And in New York, by the time you get down the elevator and outside into the street, you don't want to go back up for anything you might have forgotten.

So we're down on the street when Joy asks, "Did you remember to bring your wallet?"

I checked. No—don't have it.

And she didn't have hers, either. So there we were, without a dime between us, walking over to the video store.

She asks, "Well, what are we going to do?"

And I say, "You know, wherever I go, people come up to say hello. I will find someone who will lend me five dollars and I'll pay them back tomorrow! I tell you—it always works!"

Joy says, "You're crazy! That's ridiculous."

I say, "But I don't want to go *back* across the street, *up* in the elevator, and *down* the hall to the apartment just to get the stupid wallet! I'm sure there'll be *somebody* who'll lend me the cash!"

So we head over to Tower and, all the while, I'm scoping around for someone I know. And, sure enough, I spot a girl who works over at the Reebok gym, which is in our neighborhood. I see her there every day. I just can't remember her name! Fortunately, she recognizes me and so I tell her what my dilemma is. No problem. She hands me five singles.

Here's where the real fun begins: We decide on a movie—*Secrets and Lies*—and take it up to the counter. I hand it to the checkout guy, then whip out my five singles to pay him. But he doesn't want my cash. Turns out that if you want to rent a movie, *you first have to join their renter's club.*

And to do that, you need to show them your driver's license, a photo ID, your birth certificate, major credit card, proof of citizenship—everything but a blood sample!

Which means, yes—

You need your wallet.

So I say to the guy, "Look, I work at ABC across the street. I'm there every morning between nine and ten. Come in with the cops and arrest me if I don't get the tape back to you!"

But he's being Mr. Tough Guy. "Nope. Gotta have a photo ID and a major credit card."

Nothing I can do to convince him. So . . .

"I'll be right back!"

And . . .

I go *out* of the store . . .

And *across* the street . . .

And *into* my building . . .

And *up* in the elevator . . .

Down the hall . . .

Into the apartment.

And I find my wallet.

Then it's back *down* the hall, *down* in the elevator, *across* the street, *through* the doors, and *into* the store. But wait! Then I had to fill out the membership form—when was I born, where do I work, what's my mother's maiden name . . .

PLEASE!!

I JUST WANT TO LOOK AT A VIDEO!

So I finally get the video, go back *out* of the store again, *across* the street again, *into* the apartment building again, *up* in the elevator again, *down* the hall again, and *into* the apartment . . .

AGAIN!

And I'm *exhausted.*

This better be one terrific movie after all the trouble I went through to get it!

So we put in the movie and get comfortable.

Ten minutes into it I begin drifting off.

Couldn't stay with it.

Wasn't for me.

Started wondering what the Yankees were doing.

And I was gone.

But Joy enjoyed it very much.

The next afternoon, I have to return the video. So I head back to Tower—where, amazingly, there's only one person in line at the video counter. I figure I'll be in and out in no time. So the cashier starts ringing this guy up and I'm waiting. And waiting.

AND WAITING.

What can possibly be taking so long? I've bought cars in less time. So I take a look at what he's buying. He's got a bin full of CDs and videos. And the guy behind the counter has to scan each one *individually*. And I'm waiting. And waiting. The final total: $556.93! I just wanted to return one measly $1.87 video that *I didn't even watch.*

But that's not where this story ends. Oh, no.

When I get home, my nerves are frayed. Joy's not around, so I pour some coffee left over from that morning into a teacup. (I couldn't find any mugs!) I pop it into the microwave—forty-five seconds—start, bang, go. Usually with a mug, I reach right in, grab that sucker and drink it—no problem. But mugs are much *t-h-i-c-k-e-r* than teacups.

So I reach in and—

"AAAAGGGGHHHHHHH!!!"

I drop the teacup. Scalding coffee spills all over me, all over the floor, all over the stove and underneath the microwave. And the teacup is in smithereens. It was the good china kind, too. Which Joy ain't going to be very pleased about.

So I run and get sponges, rags, towels—I get everything. And I'm on my knees wiping and cleaning and thinking, *How am I gonna explain this?* Then I think, *Maybe I'll hide the evidence, won't say a word and wait for a more opportune time to mention it to Joy . . .*

Anyway, I worked like a *dog*. I knocked myself out on that kitchen! Left it *spotless*. Then I carefully buried the teacup at the bottom of the trash and covered it up.

I'm telling you, the place looked as clean as a whistle.

And then I waited . . . feeling *confident* that I would not be discovered.

A while later, Joy got home. She walked into the kitchen, looked around and—*I swear to God*—she said, "Regis, did you break a teacup?"

For all my scrubbing and scouring and mopping, I overlooked a small piece of the handle that slipped into a corner.

I missed it.

But her radar spotted it.

So I said, "Who, me?"

YOU GET THE **POPCORN!**

In case you care, my wallet curse continues in this story.

Thank God, it has a happy ending.

FOR A CHANGE!

But, not too long ago, we avoided a major family tragedy.

Why?

Because I'm always thinking.

Joy and I had gone to a movie premiere and, midway through the film, she leaned over to me and said, "I want some popcorn." Now, my wallet was deep in the back pocket of my pants. In order to get it, I had to lean to one side, burrow through my raincoat, reach down behind my jacket, and fish it from the back of my pants. All of which I did. Then I handed her the money, and out she went to get her popcorn—

> *JOY: You know, I'll bet a lot of people might have thought that you were going to say, "I'll get the popcorn for you, Joy." That would have eliminated going through the whole ordeal to dig out the wallet.*

No. I used to do that!

But then *Millionaire* got hot and too many people started coming up to me to say, **"Is that your final popcorn?"** I don't want to go through that anymore. I really can't take it!

Anyway, instead of fighting through the layers of clothes to put the

41

wallet back, I left it on my lap for the rest of the movie. And when we got up to leave, I heard something fall.

But I thought, *Naw, that can't be me . . . probably just Joy's popcorn container . . .*

> JOY: *Right, because* nobody *would leave his wallet in his lap at a movie theater. But you did. You felt confident that you would remember it, which you didn't.*

Can I finish this story, please?

Does anyone here understand the simple concept of dramatic momentum?

Okay. Now as we walk toward the escalator to exit the theater, I feel a little light. You know that feeling—like something's missing. I can hear my keys jangling—so I have those. Then I reach for the wallet—and it's not there.

Yes, I dropped the wallet!

But the fact that I realized I felt light proves one thing:

I'M ALWAYS THINKING!

So now I have to turn around and go back into the theater where most of the audience is still streaming out. I'm like a salmon swimming upstream! I have to fight my way back in so I can get down on my hands and knees to look for the wallet. And, you know, these theater floors are a little gamey!

> JOY: *Meanwhile, I was greeting everyone pouring out of the premiere by the escalator while I waited for you.*

No, you had vanished. You had faded into the mist.

Anyway, thank God, I found the wallet. Right there on that floor where I dropped it.

JOY: *You're one lucky guy. But I'm surprised you even found your seat again, much less your wallet. Usually when Regis has gone out for refreshments—not that this is a problem anymore—he forgets where he was sitting.*

Well, can you imagine what would have happened if I hadn't found it? All the credit card canceling and the applying for a new driver's license and every other miserable task that I have no idea how to do? There would have been quite a chill in the air that night. There would have been no talking between us. There would have been TOTAL SILENCE!

JOY: *As it was, there was little talking, if I remember correctly. But, you know, things have changed. You used to have this black cloud over your head. There was a time when you never would have found that wallet.*

Not now! Now I have BLUE SKIES!

Actually, who are we trying to kid? My black cloud is never too far away. It just needs time off once in a while to recharge.

IN AND OUT ALREADY!

When you live in a New York City apartment, you almost never have to go to a hardware store to fix anything. Usually, your building maintenance guys will do that for you. Apartment life is so much simpler. But living in a house in Connecticut is an altogether different story. You're forever running to these hardware stores. And the one where I seem to run the most is a big Caldor in Greenwich.

Now, for the longest time, this store was so disorganized, you could never find anything. And, let me tell you, there's nothing I love more than a well-organized store! For instance, I could find my way around *blind-folded* in our local IGA supermarket. Blindfolded, I can find everything I need! That's how well I know that store.

But this Caldor store was never organized. Many times, I wanted to stop and restock those shelves myself just to help them out. Finally, a few years ago, I noticed there was a team in there restocking and reordering the merchandise. By God, they got it together! Suddenly, it became a totally efficient store. It has run like a top ever since!

Except for one thing: the automatic in and out doors.

Some of the doors open and some of them don't.

When you're *leaving* the store—your arms full of packages—the doors fly open for you! Thereby allowing you an easy exit. It's the least they can do after taking your money. Anyway, one day a while ago, I was out running errands and I tried to go in one of those doors—

JOY: Wait a minute. You tried to go in *through the* out *door?*

I don't know. It said *EXIT*, but I didn't bother to read it.

So just as I tried to get in, this door flew open and almost knocked me out! A woman exited and then the door slammed shut. Then I moved over to the next door—

JOY: Which was the right door.

Yes, THE RIGHT DOOR!

So I move over to the one that says *ENTER* and go in. But, as I'm about to do just that, I see a little girl inside the store walk toward me until she's right in front of the door. So rather than go in and have that door whip open and smack this kid in the head, I quickly jump back. But the kid just stands there looking at me.

So I say, "Little girl, why don't you move away from the door so it doesn't hit you when it opens?!"

She doesn't budge, just keeps standing there, looking at me. She must have been seven or eight years old. Maybe she recognized me. I don't know, but I just didn't want to hit this kid with the door.

JOY: And she's just staring at you.

She's staring . . .
AND SHE WON'T MOVE!

Meanwhile, people are lining up behind me, waiting to get in, wondering what my problem is. It's *embarrassing!*

Then it occurs to me that maybe this door doesn't flip open automatically. So I push it and, by God, it opens!

No wonder this kid was staring at me!

She was probably wondering, *Why is that dope standing out there? Why doesn't he just open the door?*

JOY: Did you feel a little silly with all those people hovering around waiting behind you?

Of course I felt a little silly!

I said, "I'M SORRY, FOLKS! BUT THAT'S IT FOR YOUR SUNDAY SHOW HERE AT CALDOR!"

Very embarrassing.

JOY: Just for the record, Regis, can I ask you what you were doing at Caldor?

All right, I'm not too proud!

I'll be happy to tell you and everybody else:

I exchanged a mop that broke!

I don't care.

I walked in with a broken mop in my hand.

And I was in my tennis outfit to boot!

The heads of everyone in line twisted to take a look at me—

"Is that you, Regis?"

"What are you doing with that mop, Regis?"

What else could I say but—

"It broke."

That's right. I bought a mop, brought it home and found out it was broken. So I took it back, told them about it and got a new one. And *I don't care* if everyone thinks I'm crazy for doing it! Someday *you'll* have to go exchange a mop and know what it feels like to be ridiculed!

But just watch out for little kids when that store door opens.

TRAPPED AT HOME TOGETHER

I don't know why I thought it would be a good idea to spend two straight weeks of summer vacation time at home in Connecticut. Sometimes, I guess, you just get tired of flying off to different places and feel the need to spend some quality time around the house. But after what we went through during this particular vacation, all I can tell you is that I've never suggested it again!

Here was how Joy and I recapped the experience immediately afterward when she happened to be filling in as cohost on *Live!* Hold on to something . . .

J.P.: And how was *your* vacation, Regis?

ME: It was two solid weeks of TOGETHERNESS. Every day! Every night! Every second of every minute! Every minute of every hour! Together!

The second day into it, she uttered the words that I'm sure many of you ladies have said in similar situations when your husband is home and you're not used to him being there: "I can't WAIT . . . for YOU . . . to GO BACK TO WORK!!!"

J.P.: I got through two whole days before I said that.

ME: Two days! But you said it a couple of times afterward. And, each time, I bit my lip because what do I want to do, have a confrontation right there? But quietly—to myself, actually in my heart—I said, "NEITHER CAN I."

J.P.: You were the one who wanted to take three weeks off in a row, and I said, "You can't do that."

ME: Nothing but one crisis after another the whole time. On the first day, we were trying to fix the outdoor grill . . .

J.P.: Regis doesn't know anything about the grill.

ME: Don't want to learn, either.

J.P.: You can't even turn on the grill.

ME: That I can't do, you're absolutely right. But once in a while I do turn the chicken over. And I do that pretty well! But anyway, I was trying to scrape it down for you. And in order to get these holes open so that the fire comes out, I used a broom handle. When I was finished, I laid the broom on top of the rolltop hood.

Now, anybody could have seen this broom handle! But Joy, without even looking, opens the hood and the broom whacks her right in the eye, giving her a BLACK EYE!

J.P.: I had a shiner the whole time we were on vacation.

ME: I had to look at her with a black eye.

J.P.: I'm telling you right now—when you retire, I'm getting a full-time job. It is not easy to be with you!

ME: It was too much togetherness! There was no relief!

J.P.: Then Regis said, "I've got a great idea. Let's go to The Home Depot. Wouldn't that be fun? I need a lot of things."

ME: I'd never been to The Home Depot! I never have a chance to go to The Home Depot! And they have one up there in Connecticut.

J.P.: So Regis buys an eight-foot ladder that extends to sixteen feet. And also a saw. Just the thought of what he's going to do with the saw scared me to death. But the real problem was that he gave no thought to how we were going to get this ladder home. He gets it out to the car, and we're in the girls' little Acura. He looks at the car and he looks at the ladder.

And I say, "What's your plan?"

He tells me, "I have no plan!"

ME: SHE ALMOST GOT ANOTHER SHINER RIGHT THERE!

J.P.: We're in this huge parking lot, which means it's practically a two-mile walk back to the store to get a cord to tie the trunk down. So Regis walked back to get a cord, then he couldn't find any hook in the trunk to tie it to. So I had to tie it down for him. And then we drive home with this large ladder back there, going: *Boom! Boom! Boom!*

ME: Incidentally, the ladder—which we finally got home—cost about fifty bucks. But the car is now ruined.

J.P.: It was a *verrrry* long vacation, Regis.

MY CONNECTICUT CHAIN SAW MASSACRE

I'm a man of few needs. Of course, that makes it particularly hard to buy gifts for me. Whether it's birthday, Christmas, Father's Day, whatever—I mostly just want some peace and quiet. But on a Father's Day not too long ago—for the first time in a long while—I actually *wanted* something. I mean, *really wanted* something. So when J.J. and Joanna asked me, like they do every year, "Dad, what do you want for Father's Day?"—I told them the truth.

I said, **"I want a chain saw!"**

They just laughed at me.

"No way!" they said. "Too dangerous."

And Joy wasn't crazy about it, either.

But I like a little danger around me.

I'm a dangerous kind of guy.

Besides, chain saws are actually very safe if you use them correctly. I just wanted one to trim branches and cut wood at our place in Connecticut. Keep your measly little hedge clippers! Get those stupid pruning shears away from me! I'm like Abe Lincoln: I like to chop my wood proudly and manfully! I wanted to make logs!

But I was sick of using an ax. Too much effort.

With a chain saw, I could pull the rip cord, lay that blade on a tree trunk and, boom, a log would be cut. Trees are always falling all over the place up there and I wanted to be the one to carve them up. It had been a secret dream of mine for a long time.

When I mentioned my chain saw wish on the air to Kathie Lee and

Gelman, they agreed with the family: "No, Regis, definitely not." "The answer is NO." "You cannot be trusted with a chain saw!" "They're not safe." I expected that from Kathie Lee, but not from Gelman, too. What a worry wart. Kathie Lee said, "Regis, with all due respect, you can't even operate the toys we sometimes have on this show. You get frustrated, throw it down and blame Gelman."

(All right, that part's true—but I wasn't talking about a crummy little battery-operated car here. I was talking about a strong, trustworthy chain saw!)

"Never mind," I said, "I'll buy it myself. I gotta have one!"

A few days later, though, they presented me with a gift box and a card that read, "Happy Father's Day! Love, Kathie Lee, Gelman and the staff." (*When exactly did I become their father?!*) Kathie Lee said, "Remember what you've been asking for?" I thought: *This has to be some kind of joke. There's no way they'd get me a chain saw.* And do you know what? I was right. They got me some cheap plastic *toy* chain saw with a pair of safety goggles and a plastic hard hat with a light on it. Not exactly what I wanted, all right? "That's as close as you're gonna get to having a power chain saw!" Kathie Lee said, laughing it up. I ask you: IS IT SO HARD FOR ANYONE TO TAKE ME SERIOUSLY?

Then our *Live!* viewers started to weigh in on the subject, via letters and faxes:

"*Dear Regis, you have trouble operating children's toys. Have mercy. No chain saw! Chain saw and Regis equal tragedy.*"

Another: "*Regis, leave the chain saw alone or one of your favorite parts could be gone!*"

And another: "*Don't even think about getting a chain saw. Remember that black cloud that follows you when you travel? I think it goes to Connecticut, too!*"

This one, though, came from a woman who really understood me and my needs: "*Dear Regis, I'm a woman of 73 years. I never in my life wrote a letter to anyone in show business. I'm writing about the chain saw. I still climb trees to trim with my chain saw. If I can do it, so can you. Go for it! Don't let anyone treat you like a wimp! I have a gas-powered chain saw that's almost like new. If I lived in the city, I would gladly give it to you."*

I loved that lady!

Well, I begged and I pleaded and I hoped against hope and, finally, Father's Day rolled around. And let me tell you what the girls gave me: a blender.

A blender!

I once gave my grandmother a blender!

True, I'd also asked for a blender to mix up vitamins and juices. But my heart wasn't in it. Everybody has a blender. And now I, too, had a blender. It was a very nice blender and I use it all the time—but HOW WAS I SUPPOSED TO CHOP WOOD WITH A BLENDER?! I lost heart. I pitied myself. I grumbled a lot on the air: "Oh, they're probably right . . . I'd probably just cut myself and bleed to death somewhere out in the back brush."

I must have looked like a very sad case up there. Because later that year—out of the kindness of her heart—Rosie O'Donnell gave me MY CHAIN SAW! (In fact, a couple of viewers even sent me their chain saws, God bless them.) So now I was finally equipped and ready to rip up wood. I lugged it up to Connecticut one fall weekend to give it a test run. AND IT WAS THE BEST WEEKEND OF MY LIFE! Joy couldn't believe what she was witnessing.

JOY: When you came inside afterward, I hadn't seen a smile on your face like that . . . Well, maybe once, a long time ago.

No, not even then.

JOY: You were out there for hours.

Loving every minute of it.

51

I got out there, loaded it with oil and gas, pulled the rip cord and—
Vrrrooooooom! Got that sucker started! Squeezed the trigger and revved it
up a little. Loved squeezing that trigger, loved revving it up. Then I cut
everything in sight. EVERYTHING. I love cutting, absolutely adore it!

> *JOY: Regis was so proud. He had a little help, of course. He doesn't like to
> work alone.*

I had my Alfredo with me. I call him Fredo. He's our landscaping guy
up there. Fredo taught me all about chain-sawing. I got the hang of it
pretty quickly, too. I trimmed, I pruned, I buzzed through thick trees like
they were paper! So many loose logs that needed cutting, too. Big ones,
heavy ones, all of them just lying there, *disturbing my symmetrical eye!*
Blasted right through them! *Vrrrrrooomm!* I'm telling you, the chain saw
is one of the world's greatest inventions—better than Velcro!

Listen to me, all of you timid or clumsy guys out there: Don't be
afraid! Pick up that chain saw and be proud that YOU'RE A CHAIN
SAW MAN!

> *JOY: I'm jealous. I wish I had something that gave me that much pleasure.
> You know, I think you might be in the wrong business. I never see you
> come home from* Millionaire *that excited. Would you rather work with
> your chain saw or do* Millionaire?

Why can't I do both?

I could keep a chain saw on the set. And every time I get a little
bored waiting for somebody's final answer, I could reach down and rev
it up a bit. V*rooooom-vrooooom!* I tell you, it might step up the pacing
once in a while.

Anyway, my chain saw is the greatest.

And now I'm learning to juggle with it.

BETTER LIVING THROUGH COYOTE URINE

I never had anything against deer. I like how they prance and run around and wander through their leafy tree-shaded forests. They are serene, lovely creatures and I like to spot them whenever I'm driving around up in Connecticut. The only problem is this: They don't *stay* in their forests. In fact, they *refuse* to stay in their forests.

Instead, all they want to do is come out of their forests and EAT MY FLOWER BEDS!

In Greenwich, we have a nice piece of property. We love to plant things around it. Joy is always out there planting new rows of impatiens and daffodils to brighten up the yard. And the reason we're always planting new rows of flowers is because THE DEER KEEP EATING THE OLD ROWS OF FLOWERS.

It's an impossible situation and a frustrating problem all over the Northeastern United States. The deer have nothing to eat during the winter and early spring months. But in the summertime they come to devour your gardens like dessert! I can't tell you how many racks of flowers we've had to keep buying over the years. We finally built a big see-through fence around the property. And guess what?

The deer get through the fence!

Every Sunday we leave the Greenwich house with flowers blooming everywhere. And every Friday we drive back up from the city and . . .

THE FLOWERS ARE GONE!

Naturally, I've complained about this on the air and begged viewers for solutions. And, as always, they sent in all kinds of strange suggestions. But the one we had the most fun with on the show came in a little vial that contained COYOTE URINE!

Frankly, I don't know how they got coyote urine into this little bottle—and, moreover, *I don't want to know!*

But, apparently, if you sprinkle it around the edges of your flower beds, the deer will stay away, fearing they're treading on coyote territory. It makes perfect sense, too. And I really should have used it on our gardens in Greenwich.

But the truth is, never mind the deer—

I DON'T WANT TO GET ANYWHERE NEAR COYOTE URINE, EITHER!

I was afraid.

Let me keep buying new flowers every weekend, but don't make me touch coyote urine! I'm sorry, but can I retain just a little shred of dignity here?

Anyway, there's one very odd follow-up to this story:

Some time later, I took Joanna to see the famed actress Uta Hagen in an Off-Broadway play at the Lucille Lortel Theatre downtown in New York City. And Uta Hagen was something else in the show, just great. So I said, "Joanna, I want you to meet her after the show." I wasn't sure whether she even knew who I was, but I figured I would introduce myself. Joanna was thrilled.

So we waited until the theater had emptied except for the handful of us who wanted to greet her. And, finally, out came Uta Hagen, looking very regal and distinguished. She stepped down off the stage, walked up the aisle and said hello to a few people. Then she looked over toward me and screamed—

"My God! *Regis Philbin!* I've got to thank you for something. You have really saved my life!"

And I'm thinking: *I've never met this woman before in my life! What could it possibly be?*

She said, "You told me how to get rid of deer out in the Hamptons! Thank you, thank you, for telling me about *coyote piss*!"

Of course, we had talked about coyote *urine* on the show. But, by God, Uta Hagen spelled it out exactly the way it was.

And, by the way, what a thrill it is to know that whenever this great lady of the American stage might see my face on television, she immediately thinks of *coyote piss!*

I'm a lucky guy.

A VERY THORNY SUBJECT

Just call me Mr. Green-Thorns.

On second thought, please don't call me that.

But let me tell you one thing—I'm the greatest when it comes to growing roses! It's true. A couple of summers ago, I took it upon myself to plant rosebushes on one side of the property. More importantly, I actually did it without any help. And they're still there, blooming like crazy! In fact, these bushes are so beautiful, the deer won't even touch them. Of course, deer don't like thorns—but I still deserve some major credit. They are the only flowering plants of ours that continue to thrive!

Joy's daffodils—wilted and bitten away.

My roses—strong, tall, unstoppable!

I am very proud of those roses.

Anyway, the one thing we've never really done at the Connecticut place is to professionally landscape it, make it look pristine and nice.

JOY: Well, let's just say we've done it poorly.

Our problem is that you have to know which kinds of plants will do well in certain places there. You've got to know which kind of flower works in which kind of soil and so on. But then Joy learned about two guys who had successfully landscaped around another house nearby. And these guys were *serious* landscapers. Or, to spell it out for you—

E-X-P-E-N-S-I-V-E.

So on a Saturday morning not too long ago they came over to the house—and they're taking pictures, they're measuring, they're envisioning, they're sculpting. One of them was making copious notes on every single inch of our yard. Frankly, I wanted to get away when I started hearing them say things like:

"This is going to be a *big one* . . . "

And: "We're going to have to put a *forest* over here . . . "

JOY: "Wouldn't it be nice to have a sculpture and a fountain over there . . . "

And: "Yes, yes, a *fountain* right there. *Absolutely!* And it's going to have to be a *very big fountain!*"

Suddenly, all I could see was the national debt growing in our yard instead of trees and plants!

JOY: But we're going to get an estimate, Regis, and if you don't like it,
we're going to do it anyway.

I'm going to fight you on that one, because I could just sense from these guys that it would be a BIG, BIG ESTIMATE.

JOY: But, as you said, it's a long time coming. It's time.

No, it's NOT time! I changed my mind.

And here's why:

Over and over, I kept pointing out my flourishing rosebushes to them. They didn't care. They smiled at me and looked away—every time! Then, after all of their measuring and envisioning, they said, "You know what would look really good here? *Some rosebushes.*"

I said, "But I did that over there! *By myself.*"

He didn't want to know about those—he wanted *other* rosebushes!

For $20,000, the only thing he told me was to put in more rose-bushes!

I don't think so.

Plus, the deer would starve.

CAN WE PLEASE STOP REDECORATING?

Please feel my pain.

Joy—as host of her own home-decorating show, *Haven*—has a never-ending mission at the Connecticut house. And that mission is to drive her Regis crazy by changing and rotating every single stick of furniture there *on a weekly basis!* Maybe she sees it as ongoing research for *Haven.* Maybe she never wants me to know where anything is in our own home.

Let me give you an idea of the madness, from a morning exchange not long ago on *Live!* . . .

J.P.: Yesterday I spent the whole day up in Connecticut waiting for the last piece of new furniture, which I ordered in November. It's April now. You would think I'd have a little pull by hosting a home-furnishing program, but I don't.

ME: You tell them, "This is JOY PHILBIN FROM *HAVEN* . . ." And they say, "Yeah, so?"

J.P.: I was waiting and waiting. The guy told me to be there at eleven o'clock sharp. He said the delivery men won't wait. At two-thirty, my decorator girlfriend Katherine Stevens and I were still waiting. Thank God, she was there—we got a lot accomplished. Because apparently the truck broke down on the Tappan Zee Bridge. So we decided to push around a lot of furniture. We hung a lot of pictures. Nothing that you will notice when you get up there, of course. But I was exhausted when I got back to New York. Every muscle in my body ached.

ME: Yeah, but besides that, I'm sorry to hear that you pushed around furniture. Katherine and Joy go up there once a week and move a couch from here to over there. A stool from here to over there. All they do is move furniture back and forth from this room to that one. And just when I'm warming up to one arrangement, it's gone! It's over there now! *Where? Where?*

J.P.: And, meanwhile, all you have to do all day is sit there and say, "Now you've got two more lifelines. Which one do you want to use?" You're making the big bucks. And I'm up there shoving furniture around.

ME: Yeah, and if I wasn't saying, "You have two lifelines," you wouldn't have any FURNITURE TO MOVE!!

J.P.: Well, maybe I should get some new furniture.

ME: THERE'S NO MORE ROOM FOR ANY MORE FURNITURE!

J.P.: That's true—it's beginning to look like a warehouse.

ME: I can't take it anymore! *Joy! When does it end?*

WHO WANTS TO BE A HANDYMAN?

This has turned into the longest-running joke in the family.
AND FRANKLY, I'M SICK OF IT.
Do you hear me?
S-I-C-K OF IT!

Apparently, it's not enough to single-handedly save a network and cohost a successful morning talk show. No, not nearly enough! As a strapping example of American manhood—*I'm also supposed to be useful around the house!*

Well, I've said it before and I'll say it again:

I'm not handy.

You want handy? Go find Bob Vila. You don't even want me to try. Before Joy and I were married, my own mother warned her: "I raised him like a fine piece of crystal. Don't screw it up."

> JOY: *She was absolutely right. That explains why you don't know how to do anything around the house. She never even asked you to screw in a lightbulb, did she?*

She wouldn't dare.

The way I've always seen it is this: Whatever you don't learn how to do, you don't have to do. AND I DON'T WANT TO HAVE TO DO THINGS I'M NOT GOOD AT.

But, by the way, I'm not completely helpless:

I used to know how to work the coffeemaker.

Then I forgot. (And I'm not kidding.)

Garbage disposal—a breeze!

I'm the greatest at clearing plates off a table!

And I can turn on—and *also* empty—a vacuum and an electric broom.

> JOY: *Wait one second. I have a story about that. This was something that happened at the Connecticut house not long ago. There was a mess on the carpet in front of our fireplace because we had left the flue open during high winds. I said to Regis, "I'm going out and—if you're not watching sports or anything—could you take the electric broom and clean up those ashes?" When I came home, the whole broom was in*

pieces on the kitchen floor. He had put it on top of the counter and tried to empty the container of dust. But of course it fell down and broke into several pieces.

Not my fault! Somebody's gotta empty it once in a while. The broom fell down and it broke—big deal!

JOY: Now we have no broom.

That's what you're going to get for Christmas.

JOY: Can I share another classic Regis moment? I'm sorry, Regis. I shouldn't tell this, but I have to. One night in the apartment I watched him try to change the lightbulb in a lamp over and over. He must have changed it four times, and it still didn't work right. "This darn lamp!" he said. "I'm gonna have to take it in and get it fixed because it's dim no matter what type of bulb I use." So I walked over, flipped the dimmer switch and the light went on—full intensity. He said, "How did you do that?" I told him, "There's a dimmer switch right here on the wall."

It was an honest mistake. I put four different bulbs in there. **FOUR DIFFERENT BULBS!** It didn't work! Couldn't figure it out! I was going crazy! Turned out somebody put the dimmer down. And if I find out *who* put that dimmer down, they're gonna get it!

JOY: You're just lucky you're married to a handy woman. The trouble is that the problem-solving side of your brain never really developed. Somehow or other you got shortchanged.

I did. I got shortchanged. But I'm not *that* unhandy! I'm tired of your complaints, Joy! Really sick and tired!

JOY: *I'm not complaining. I'm just pointing out the truth. You have to admit that the light switches are a perfect example.*

Well, light switches are tough! I'll bet you didn't know that I once turned on every light in the house ALL BY MYSELF!

JOY: *I'm very proud of you, Regis.*

That's all I wanted to hear.

Take Me OWWWWT TO THE BALLGAME

I'm a diehard Yankees fan. What do you expect from a guy who grew up in the Bronx? Every time I set foot in The House That Ruth Built, I'm always genuinely humbled. And it's a great thrill to be occasionally invited to sit in owner George Steinbrenner's private box, where you feel like you're up on top of baseball's premiere cathedral. You can't help but gaze down on that field and imagine you see the ghosts of Joe D, Gehrig, Mantle and the Bambino all running around those base paths one more time.

Anyway, not long ago, the dream of a lifetime came true for me: I got to suit up with my Yankees during spring training in Tampa.

I happened to be on a Florida nightclub tour with Don Rickles and thought—*Why not drop by Legends Field to see the guys getting ready for the new season?* Steinbrenner built this beautiful little stadium complex for his minor-league franchise and for the Yankees to train. Everywhere you look there are practice fields and nothing but Yankees—all in their pinstripes—tossing, catching and swinging at balls. Late-afternoon Florida sun glints down on that green grass. And you just know that all the worries these guys might have stay outside the gates of this place. It's quite a picture.

Once I got there, it didn't take long before I was invited to go put on a uniform in manager Joe Torre's office. And let me tell you what a thrill it was to climb into those pinstripes! And then I walked out onto the field a little starry eyed. Of course, Yankee fans were there in the stands, yelling and making noise . . . *and very surprised to see me striding out onto that diamond.*

"HEY, REGIS, IS THAT YOUR FIIIIIIII—"

I'm sorry, but I had to tune them out!

I had no time for that nonsense.

Not now!

I was a Yankee now!

And we had a big season to prepare for!

I walked over to the batting cage and Joe Torre said, "Regis, would you like to hit a few?" Great former sluggers like Reggie Jackson and Chris Chambliss were standing around the cage, ready to observe. Coach Willie Randolph was pitching batting practice. Nervously, I took a bat and stepped up to the plate. It had been a long time since I'd swung a bat. And now I had the Yankees of yesterday, today and tomorrow all watching me!

I felt terribly inept.

But I got hold of a couple pitches and slapped them not very deep into the outfield. To me, though, they felt like big home runs. Coach Bill Robinson pointed out that I was hitting flat-footed, not rising up on my toes. He said, "Come up on your back foot." Which I did and sure enough I got more distance.

I was whacking the balls deeper and deeper.

Which was when I got a little cocky—started yelling and screaming, as I am wont to do.

"OKAY, HERE I GO! HEY, WATCH THIS, REGGIE!!"

I'm shooting my mouth off . . .

"THIS ONE'S GOING OUT!!!"

I can't shut up . . .

"I SAVED THE ABC TELEVISION NETWORK AND NOW I'M HERE TO SAVE THE YANKEES, BABY!"

And here came the next pitch . . . and I swung . . . and hit it foul directly off my right shin!

Well, it hurt. Boy, did it hurt.

It stung and smarted. I could feel it swelling.

But I was so energized by being out there with these guys that I just continued to take a few more swings.

Then I stepped out of the cage . . .

And my shin began to throb.

And throb.

AND THROB!

I went back to Joe's office and pulled down those socks. And there was this nasty black welt rising up on my leg. There was a tear in the skin, too. Ouch! Yankee trainer Gene Monahan came right in and put ice on it. He took a good look at the shin and said, "Regis, you've got a *wound* there!"

A wound!

I mean, that's all I had to hear.

That night, I went back to see the Yankees play and limped up to Steinbrenner to show him my shin. I said, "George, I love you, but if this welt is still here tomorrow—I GOT A PIECE OF THE YANKEES! I'm sorry!" That had him laughing. Sure, George, go ahead and laugh!

Meanwhile, my welt kept growing until it wasn't a welt anymore. It was a bump.

A big ugly bump.

A couple of days later, Joy flew down to meet me in Palm Beach so that we could spend some time together.

> JOY: I had arrived earlier while Regis was out performing his act with
> Don Rickles. We'd hoped to play a lot of tennis together while I was
> down there. So I'd brought my tennis racket and reserved courts for

*the next morning. And Regis came limping into the room at about
eleven o'clock at night: "I had an accident. I'm injured. I can't
play."*

I got no sympathy at all!

She had her cute little tennis skirt and was ready to play. I said, "I
don't think I can. This thing is throbbing and hurting and aching!"
Naturally, I thought she'd say, "Oh, my gosh! What a terrible wound! I'm
so worried about you!"

Instead I got this:

"You're *kidding* me! You can't play tennis?!"

I ask you:

WHERE WAS THE SYMPATHY?

I had sustained this gruesome Major League Baseball injury—*and I
got nothing but attitude!*

*JOY: First of all, I don't understand why you couldn't have just stayed in
the stands and watched the game like everybody else. Why did you
feel the need to go down onto the field and pretend like you were
twenty-five years old?*

Are you kidding?

And pass up a chance to get in the New York Yankees batting cage
with Reggie and Chris Chambliss and all those guys watching?

JOY: The ball could have hit you in the head and the Millionaire *show
would have gone down!*

Notice that when the breadwinning is involved, then she worries.

Anyway, in search of some real sympathy, I unveiled my shin as soon
as I got back on the air at *Live!* In fact, I happily showed it day after day,

so we could all watch together as the wound developed and got bigger and more alarming. It became a national wound.

> **ME:** . . . I'll tell you what's really scary—this bump on my leg!

> **K.L:** Oh, Regis!

> **ME:** I'm not through with this yet!

> **K.L:** You are the biggest wimp.

> **ME:** I am not a wimp! This is a WOUND! I'm taking it very seriously and, like I said, if that bump is still here on Tuesday, I'm part owner of the Yankees. Today is Tuesday and guess what—the BUMP IS STILL THERE!

> **K.L:** That is a bad-looking leg.

> **ME:** Look at this! This is serious!

> **K.L:** That leg looks like a ham hock.

> **ME:** Oh my God, it stings and it hurts.

> **K.L:** I wouldn't show that thing on national TV.

> **ME:** Well, it's good for the lawsuit. Yeah, I'm gonna have my own box at Yankee Stadium!

Well, I tried to be brave and stoic about it . . .

For the most part.

And that same week—*even though I continued to be in tremendous throbbing pain!*—I was back taping more *Millionaire* shows, which usually go on much longer than the hour broadcasts you see at home. With so much money on the line, the contestants are encouraged to take their time up there in the hot seat. Most of them do. In fact, some of them can *really . . . take . . . their . . . time!* (So much of that waiting is edited from the version that goes out on the air, otherwise you wouldn't believe what marathons these shows often become.)

So, in order to avoid discomfort, I thought I should somehow keep my bump protected during the tapings. I mentioned to one of our producers, Wendy Roth, that the doctor had advised moist heat.

She asked me, "What are you doing for it now?" I told her that I was taking ice packs out of our freezer at home and boiling them in hot water—and then putting them on my shin. She said, "I've got something better for you."

She brought me these hand warmers that—when you shake them—contain chemicals that instantly start to heat up. Not moist heat, but I figured, in a pinch, it would do the trick. She said it was probably best not to keep it on for longer than twenty minutes at a time. So I slipped this hand warmer under a kneesock right up against my shin, then began the show.

After a while, in fact, I forgot that it was there.

Now, we're in the middle of an important round with a guy who is cautiously fighting his way toward a million dollars. He's being very deliberate, very careful, weighing his options, searching the back of his mind, remembering old college classes, thinking of certain books that he's read, processing information, considering his lifelines, stroking his jaw, wringing his hands . . .

And I suddenly realize:

MY LEG IS ON FIRE!

I'm burning up!

The heat is *burrowing* into my wound!

The heat feels like it's *searing my flesh!*

AND . . . IT'S . . . KILLING ME!

Okay, I *know* I wasn't supposed to leave the warmer thing on for more than twenty minutes.

I just forgot!

But what am I supposed to do now?

Interrupt him?

"Excuse me, sir. What are you up to now? $250,000? I'll be right with you."

I can't do that!

Meanwhile, he's pondering away:

"*Hmmmmm . . . hmmmmmmmm . . . . hmmmmmmmmmmmm.*"

And I'm gritting my teeth and thinking to myself:

AAAAAGGGGGGGHHHHHHHHHH!!

Frankly, I can't remember how much money he won that night, but I can promise you this much:

That hot seat has never been any hotter than the host seat was during that show!

Meanwhile, to this day, I can still feel the remnants of that bump on my shin . . . it's still there.

(Are you listening, George?)

WHEN NOTRE DAME LOSES. . .

You don't want to talk to me.

You don't want to be near me.

You don't want to begin to understand my pain.

It's just that bad.

The truth is, nothing tears me up like a Notre Dame football loss. I was an undergraduate there majoring in psychology when—on a dark, dismal, rainy day in 1950—Purdue stormed into our stadium and handed Notre Dame its first loss in five years. *Five years of winning and never losing!* The whole student body had no concept of defeat. Never experienced it or considered it an option. We were all numb that day. We were just devastated. I remember how a bunch of us wandered over toward the team's dressing room afterward—we were lost souls, didn't know what else to do with ourselves—and the legendary head coach Frank Leahy stepped outside to talk to us. His teams had known triumph, and only triumph, for so long. But now he was going to explain defeat to us. Help us to understand it. Help us to accept it and know that adversity—on a football field and in life—only strengthens us. As a motivator, he could make the hair on the back of your neck stand up when he spoke. And that day was no exception.

It was, by far, the most important speech that I have ever heard in my life. In fact, the great coach's words would stick with me and get me through many dark patches in the decades that followed.

But nevertheless—

I CAN'T STAND IT WHEN NOTRE DAME LOSES!

Every year, I live and die with that Fighting Irish team.

Every year, I go back to that beautiful Indiana campus—it's a personal pilgrimage to hallowed ground for me. As you approach the university, you spot the Sacred Heart steeple in the distance, the Golden Dome looming above it, the two shimmering lakes . . . It's a majestic sight. You feel the tradition, the history, the ghosts of legends past. I've traveled to some of the great places in the world. But, for me, there's no better place than that campus. Those fifteen hundred acres mean everything to me. Once you are touched by the spirit of this place, it becomes part of your soul!

> *JOY: That's where Regis wants to have his ashes scattered one day. He wants to spend eternity at Notre Dame. It's that meaningful to him, but I also think it appeals to his economic side.*

I love that place!

And I'm so proud that J.J. graduated there and now Joanna is studying law at Notre Dame. It keeps me coming back year after year after year. I've been able to spend time with teams coached by Ara Parseghian, Lou Holtz and Bob Davie. I've gotten up at pep rallies, during good times and bad, and yelled and screamed and tried to stir things up.

During tough periods, I've told the team and the student body: "Look, you've got to know by now that teams from other schools used to come to Notre Dame and be awed by the Dome, by the stadium, by the legends of Rockne and the Gipper and the Four Horsemen. But not anymore. Now, they can't wait to get here. You know why? Because they know that if they win, it's the biggest game of their lives! Biggest game of their careers! It's the game they'll be talking about fifty years from now! And we can't let them have that! We must not let them have that!"

But those losses do come every once in a while.

Sometimes a little more often than I can stand.

And that's when you don't want to be near me.

JOY: That's very true.

J.J.: Oh, God, it's really bad.

JOANNA: You don't even want to know.

That's when I'm unable to talk.

I just sulk.

I know it's immature and wrong.

But I feel sick inside.

I feel DEVASTATED!

I'm sorry, Coach Leahy—

I JUST CAN'T HELP IT!

I don't even want to talk about this anymore, if you don't mind.

I mean it.

In fact, I'm wondering . . .

WHY EXACTLY DID WE EVER HAVE TO BRING ANY OF THIS UP IN THE FIRST PLACE?

Don't worry—I'll be all right again in a few minutes.

NOT THE LUCK OF THE IRISH

A STORY FROM J.J. PHILBIN:

When I was a senior in high school, I began thinking about applying to Notre Dame. I'd only been there a couple times before, but one weekend that fall, Dad took me back so that I could check it out as a prospective student. Before we got there, I said to him, "Whatever you do, please don't embarrass me." He said, "Oh, come on! I just want to show you around the place." And I said, "That's fine. But, really, I don't want to see it through your eyes. I need to take it all in for myself, so just let me do my own thing." "No problem— I'll give you as much space as you want."

It happened to be a football weekend, and that Friday night there was going to be a pep rally at the Convocation Center, which sounded exciting and fun. He was going to speak at the rally, so we walked over there and the place was packed with 18,000 people. I had no idea what was going on, so I asked him, "All right, Dad, should I go into the bleacher stands? Remember, I just want to be low profile and blend in." He said, "No, no, no, no—I have an escort for you, someone who's going to take care of you while I'm doing the pep rally." And all I could think was: Oh, no.

He walks me up to Rick Mirer, the star quarterback of the team! I'm sixteen and he's this huge, hulking older guy who says, "Hi, J.J., welcome to

71

Notre Dame! Come with me." So my dad disappears and now it's just me and Rick and he leads me straight into the locker room where coach Lou Holtz is literally doing the Xs and Os on the chalkboard and outlining plays. It's just me alone with the Notre Dame football team! I'm so embarrassed. Every player's neck is craning toward me and they're all whispering, "Who's that?" "What's she doing here?"

And I thought, This is terrible. All I wanted was a little anonymity and here I am being stared at by the whole team! *Lou is giving this motivational speech, he's gaining momentum, and finally he hits his crescendo— "GO IRISH!!!" And, all of a sudden, everybody leaps out of their chairs and starts running toward the door. I said to Rick Mirer, "What am I supposed to do now?" And he said, "Just come with me."*

So the next thing I know, we're running down this long tunnel—the Notre Dame football team and me! I don't know where we're going or what's happening, but suddenly the door flies open and we are now running out into the Convocation Center with 18,000 screaming fans and I hear my father announcing, "THE NOTRE DAME FOOTBALL TEAM!"

And here I am, this tiny girl running with the team. Oh, it was insane and mortifying. *And then he introduced the team one by one and each player stood up, until I was the only person left sitting there next to them. Everyone in the stands was pointing at me—"Who is that girl?" "Is that the new kicker?" "What does she do?"*

I wanted to crawl under a rock.

Afterward, I went up to my dad with tears in my eyes, I was so embarrassed. But he was just beaming—bursting with pride and adrenaline and spirit. So he said to me, "Well, wasn't that the biggest thrill of your life!?"

He thought he did me the world's biggest favor. But I was just dying inside. And all I could say was: "No!! I never want to come here again."

Well, she did go to Notre Dame. Not only that, but she loved it even more than I did, if that is possible. And about that night: I had been told not to worry about J.J.—that she would be well taken care of during the rally. I had no idea that the next time I saw her, she would be surrounded by all those big football players and running arm-in-arm with Rick Mirer as the crowd sang "Notre Dame, Our Mother." It was such an emotional moment. When I think about it, even *I* have to fight back tears. The place has a way of affecting the Philbins, I guess.

THE SECRET SHAME OF NET MAN!

I am Net Man!
Net Man is a stomping, crushing, lethal tennis machine!
My opponents are my meat.
AND I DESTROY MY MEAT!
I have to—because I am Net Man.
Well, I try to be, anyway.
Tennis is the only game I play anymore—but sometimes I wonder if I'm really cut out for it. I have a problem with patience. I have an even bigger problem with losing. And then there are those aches and pains afterward. Following a weekend of tennis, there are some Monday mornings when I can barely move. And I don't recover as quickly as I used to, which means soreness for days. Maybe I should just quit this game once and for all before it's too late.

> JOY: *What's it going to be like when we get* really *old? When Regis gets in and out of bed, you should hear him grunt and groan—OHHHH, OHHHHHHHHHHHH. I used to think that he was having romantic dreams.*

I wish I were!
Getting out of bed can be a real killer. There have been times when I thought I had a broken back after too much tennis. MAJOR BACK

PROBLEMS YOU COULDN'T EVEN BEGIN TO FATHOM. And I'm not kidding about that. Another man would be in bed for a month. But I'm a medical marvel. Half the time, I'm actually walking around with a broken back. And it's not funny!

> JOY: It can't be that bad. Every time someone calls and wants to play tennis, Regis says, "Yeah, let's go play!" He forgets all about the pain. It seems to just disappear.

Oh, it's still there, believe me!

But I am Net Man! When duty calls, Net Man answers! Besides, I've learned how to use injuries to lull my opponents into a false sense of security. I just keep moaning, "Oh, my back! My leg! My hamstring!" And then they ease up a little bit. And when they do, *I crush them!* But I'd rather be a good winner than a good loser.

I'M SORRY, BUT I CAN'T STAND TO LOSE!

I get so embarrassed by this. But I'm a perfectionist. I hate myself for making stupid mistakes. I can't even count the number of times I've yelled and screamed and conducted myself in a very unsportsmanlike manner. I'm not proud of it—that's just the way it is. And Joy is usually mortified by my behavior.

> JOY: Oh, it is terrible. Regis just goes berserk! And I don't even want to say how many rackets he's broken over the years. The only good thing about it is that I always know what to get him for his birthday every year. His birthday is in late August, and by the time we've gone through the summer, I know that at least one or two rackets will have bitten the dust.

It's the sad truth!

When my temper gets the best of me, heads up! Rackets will fly and crash! I'm sorry. It's uncontrollable. *I can't help it!* John McEnroe has nothing on me.

It all began about thirty years ago when I was playing at the Trousdale home of our friend Andy Sidaris in Beverly Hills. After missing a key shot, I got so disgusted with myself that I just lost control and threw my racket—which sailed twenty feet into the air and landed on the next-door neighbor's roof! And that's exactly where it stayed. For years. Every time we went back to play, Andy and his wife Arlene would look up there and laugh. It turned into some kind of monument to my stupid hotheadedness.

And the worst part of it is, that incident taught me nothing!

Because over the next three decades, I've busted racket after racket— all good ones, all bent and broken. For a long time, I used to play exclusively with Weed rackets—big, beautiful oversized models made by a small company in Ohio. They loved it when I mentioned them on the air. Every time I'd break a racket, they'd send me a new one. The last racket they sent was a special model that had been discontinued. But they saved it for me and even had an inscription etched on it: "Relax, Regis. Breathe deeply. Don't get upset."

I tried to relax. I breathed deeply. I tried not to get upset.

That one ended up smashed against an adobe wall in Scottsdale.

Most recently, I had been playing with a big, beautiful Prince racket and broke that one as well. I told the story on *Live!*—"I am just sick of it, sick of it, sick of it! I'm losing it! There's no point anymore! My temper is officially out of control on the tennis court! Broke another one yesterday." Two days later, Prince sent me three new rackets. I wrote them a thank-you letter and, because it was winter, I waited for a trip to California so that I could try one out. I took the best of the three—a gorgeous extra-wide model.

And in the very first game, I got a little angry at myself and—BAM— I just gave the court a small whack. Nothing major. But I heard that sound and thought, *Oh, my God—don't tell me! I couldn't have . . .*

But I did.

I was so embarrassed.

So furious at myself for doing it again!

I didn't want another person to know what a dope I was.

So I just finished the game with a broken racket without telling any-body.

I really have to rethink this game.

No Rest for THE WEARY

Here, in a nutshell, is the story of my life asleep—a random exchange with Kathie Lee after returning from a few days of *Live!* broadcasts at Walt Disney World . . .

> **K.L.:** We flew back through the most torrential weather. The sky was so full of electrical storms. But nothing bothered Reege. He was out cold, thank you very much. But, Reege—what a snoring problem you've got! It was unbelievable!

> **ME:** Honest to God, I didn't even know I fell asleep.

> **K.L.:** I've never heard anything like it in my life.

> **ME:** Aw, come on.

> **K.L.:** No!

> **ME:** You sound like somebody I know.

K.L.: Really?

ME: Joy.

K.L.: My sympathies to her. The woman's a saint!

Okay, it's all true. I admit it.

Everything about sleep is a tragedy for me—and a horrible inconvenience for everybody else. (And—*yes*—especially for Joy.) I'm hopeless when it comes to sleep.

The sad truth:

I sleep lightly and never very well.

Plus, there's that little problem of getting up and going to the bathroom several times a night.

Does anyone care?

No, THEY JUST COMPLAIN ABOUT ME.

As hard as I try, I don't remember what it feels like to get a good night's sleep. And, believe me, I try and try and try. For instance, whenever I try to slip off into a soft beautiful slumber, something—*or someone*—snaps me right out of it. Whether it's my nightly phone call from Gelman or it's Joy rustling around the bedroom, I don't have a chance.

Here's one thing I believe with all my heart:

In a happy marriage, people should protect each other. If one person is asleep (*like me, maybe*), the other should ensure that person's sleep by all means possible.

JOY: By which means would those be?

By being quiet. By turning off the TV. By turning off the lights. By creeping into bed. You know—*shhhhhhhhhhh.*

JOY: It's all about you, isn't it, Regis?

Only when I fall asleep, it is.

JOY: That's certainly true. You know who I admire? People who can just
crawl into bed and not do anything—not read, not watch television—
just lie down, close their eyes and go to sleep.

Those are people with free minds. Those are lucky people. And I
want to be one of them soon! Truth is, I don't even know whether or not
I'm asleep anymore. It could be some kind of disease I have.

JOY: Every time he falls asleep, I have to give him verification. He interro-
gates me: "Did I sleep? How long? Did I snore? What do you think?"
He does it all the time.

I'm going to have to see a doctor about it. I sleep like a baby for about
twenty-three minutes. And it's great sleep, solid sleep. And then I wake
up and can't get *back* to sleep. It drives me nuts! They say that sleep
cycles occur every ninety minutes—and once you miss a sleep cycle,
then you're up for another ninety minutes!

So when that happens—which is too often—I usually head to the
kitchen for my old standby. I go for my Ritz crackers with a little peanut
butter and Smucker's strawberry jam. I don't know why, but it always
seems to help.

JOY: I always know when Regis can't sleep, because when I get up in the
morning, there are little droplets of jam all over the kitchen counter.

It's my private little refuge. Only thing is, sometimes I climb back
into bed too soon, and my throat's still filled with peanut butter. It sits

right there, about mid-esophagus, choking me to death! Between my gagging and my snoring, it's no fun for Joy anymore.

> JOY: *And then there are those nights when your snoring sounds exactly like gagging anyway. Sometimes you seem to just stop breathing altogether and, just when I want to call a paramedic, you give a very loud sputtering snort. It can be quite alarming!*

See what I mean?

OKAY, SO TRAFFIC PUTS ME TO SLEEP

(Note: Lately, something has happened. I can now fall asleep even when I'm not supposed to. Listen to this . . .)

A STORY FROM JOY PHILBIN:

This happened very recently. In fact, it was the day after Gelman's wedding in the Hamptons. It had been an eventful few days for Regis, beginning with the bachelor party Thursday night. Then he was a groomsman at the Saturday night wedding. And we had been Claudia Cohen's houseguests that weekend as well. So there we were in the Sunday-afternoon Hamptons traffic, returning to the city. And it was bumper-to-bumper, stop-and-go. I was in the front passenger seat reading a magazine and J.J. and Joanna were in the backseat. And we had been just crawling along for at least forty minutes. All of a sudden, the traffic broke and everyone started to go. But we weren't moving at all. And then we started to veer very slowly to the right. I looked over and saw that Regis was sound asleep. His eyes were closed!

And, of course, we all screamed. He had been so exhausted and then bored by the traffic that he'd just forgotten where he was. So I had to take the wheel and drive the rest of the way home. We were just grateful that he fell asleep with his foot on the brake instead of on the gas pedal. Then we would have all been in trouble.

It was one time, though, that a little snoring might have been helpful as an alert.

SUE ME, BUT I SNORE!

At this point, it's no secret, either!

Frankly, I'm tired of talking about it on the air.

Frankly, I'm tired anyway.

But here we go again . . .

Understand this much—I hate that I snore. But it's almost an unsolvable problem and one that goes on and on. It truly is a male curse. I guess, according to medical studies, certain tissues will invariably vibrate in the back of our throats when we sleep. Some vibrate louder than others. Apparently, I just happen to have louder throat tissues than *everyone else in the world.*

OR SO I'M TOLD.

Repeatedly.

JOY: I have tape recordings of the sounds he makes. Years ago, I played one snoring-Regis tape when I cohosted on AM Los Angeles *with him. But he wasn't in true form that night. That was minor compared to the standard nightly performance. I want to do it again so that everyone can witness it.*

I don't think that's really necessary!

Lately, Joy has even started taking pictures of me snoring—which is really going too far! She loves to catch me with my mouth hanging open in these full-blown snoring attacks. It's *intrusive*—and very embarrassing!

> *JOY: Actually, those were our vacation photos. He just happened to fall asleep a lot when we were in the Mediterranean, mostly because of the jet lag. I thought it would be nice for him to see what he was sleeping through—sort of like a keepsake.*

It's bad, I know.

I would love to give her the gift of no more snoring. And I'm sorry about it. I know what she's hearing and it ain't pretty. I wish I could stop. But I can't. Which means there are many nights when she gets up and goes to sleep in another room.

But not before she wakes me up to tell me to stop it!

That's now truly become the worst part for me: It used to be that Joy would tell me the next morning about how loud I was snoring and how she can't take it anymore.

NOW SHE TELLS ME WHILE IT'S HAPPENING!

I get those *Big Nudges* right in the middle of my sleep.

Keep in mind that I get up four or five times a night anyway *without her hitting me!* Add to that the four or five times she gives me a sharp poke—

AND I'M AWAKE TEN TIMES A NIGHT!

No wonder I'm always exhausted.

YES, LADY, IT'S ME SNORING

I guess I've been known to fall asleep in public places. It happens during movies. It happens during Broadway shows. I'm sorry—it just happens! But there was one incident in Florida that I'll never live down. I fell asleep in Saks Fifth Avenue in Boca Raton. Joy knows that shopping is at the top of my list of Things I Hate to Do. It's bad enough that I have to shop with her in various ports while we're on cruise vacations. So I do my best to avoid it the rest of the time.

> JOY: *It's something you dread. I guess it's your worst nightmare. But we happened to be in Fort Lauderdale for a Chrissie Evert tennis tournament cosponsored by Jaguar. And the Jaguar people said, "You really should take this brand-new lovely little red convertible out for a spin. See how you like it." And I thought,* Where better to go than the mall? Might as well take Regis. *And so we went to the Saks shoe department. My favorite place.*

Women's shoes . . . I'm telling you, it was so bewildering, so mind-boggling. Women walking, running! Racing! Ripping open boxes!

> JOY: *Well, they were having a sale, Regis.*

It was FRENETIC! After a while, I couldn't take it anymore. So I sat down, very quietly, on one of the store's nice couches. Closed my eyes for just an instant—and actually fell asleep! Can't fall asleep at home, but give me a noisy store full of crazed women and I'm out like a light!

> JOY: *I didn't want to wake him. I figured the longer I left him dozing there, the more time I'd have to shop. Because Regis has a very short attention span in stores.*

Especially for women's shoes . . .

> JOY: *But, I have to tell you, I felt sorry for him, because his mouth was wide open the entire time. And the word went around the store very*

> *quickly. I had wandered off to another end of the store and I over-*
> *heard two salesladies talking about him like he was Santa Claus.*
> *"Regis is here! Did you go see him? Why don't we both go see him?*
> *He's just sitting there snoring!"*

Yes, sitting there with my MOUTH OPEN! I guess people were coming up, looking at me, having a laugh, then walking away.

> *JOY: So when you finally woke up, a woman all the way from the second*
> *floor who worked at Elizabeth Arden had come down to get a look.*
> *Regis saw this woman in a white coat and immediately said, "I've got*
> *such a neckache. Could you just give me a little massage?"*

Absolutely! She took me up and gave me a quick rub. At least, I got something for all that public humiliation. Which, by the way, was probably the best sleep I'd had in months.

It made me appreciate women's shoes in a whole new way:

Zzzzzzzzzzzzzzz . . .

BONKOS FOR SEINFELD

Have I told you that I don't sleep well at night? (All right. I know, I know.) But nothing works. Pills leave me hungover. Joy once suggested we consider getting something called a Relaxation Fountain for the bedroom. This fountain supposedly trickles gently throughout the night and sends you drifting off into a sea of tranquility. Let me tell you where that fountain would make me drift—*straight to the bathroom!*

Repeatedly. And, frankly, that's part of the problem already! The truth is, the only thing that has ever properly lulled me into a gentle state of calm and serenity is watching *Seinfeld* at eleven o'clock every night. In my opinion, it's the premiere television series of our time and of this generation. When *Seinfeld* is on, and George and Kramer and Elaine and Jerry are all caught up in their neurotic schemes, I can relax. It's the perfect ending to a day. And maybe, if I'm lucky, near the end of the show I might doze off and fall asleep, which is a blessing for me.

I've known Jerry Seinfeld for a number of years. He's been a guest on *Live!* and I think he likes the show. He once even said that Kathie Lee and I did "nothing" better than anyone he knows. Now, I *think* that was a great compliment, since his show was famously about just that—nothing. We even guest-starred on an episode once. It was the one where Kramer comes on our show to hawk a silly coffee table book that looked like a miniature coffee table. Classic episode. Except that there was one tragic flaw: When Kramer comes out and starts wreaking havoc, the *Seinfeld* writers wanted me to exclaim, **"This guy is *bonkos!*"**

Not bonkers, mind you.

Bonkos.

I don't understand *bonkos.*

Have you ever heard of anyone being referred to as *bonkos?*

Neither have I.

It had to be a mistake. Before the filming, I called the *Seinfeld* writers and said, "*Bonkos?* Is this funny? I've never said bonkos in my life." They told me, "Yes, Regis. We want you to say *bonkos.* We think it'll be very funny!"

Can I tell you how hilarious *bonkos* is?

Three times they made me say it in that episode. THREE TIMES! *"This guy is bonkos!" "You're bonkos, Kramer!" "I tell you, he's bonkos!"* Right there in front of a live studio audience, no less. And let me tell you—**not one laugh**. NOT ONE! Not even a hiccup. They let me hang! They let me die!

I happen to be the only guy in history who never got a laugh on *Seinfeld*! It's very embarrassing, considering I have to watch it in reruns again and again.

I remember one night when Joy and I were out to dinner with some people. And who happens to come up to the table but none other than the man himself, Jerry Seinfeld, with his then future wife Jessica Sklar. We visited for a while and I congratulated him again on his great show. In fact, I told him that I was going right home to watch the syndicated repeat at eleven o'clock. I told him, "I've gotta get my *Seinfeld* fix or I can't sleep." So I tuned in and there it was: The dreaded Coffee Table Book episode! And there I was—*bonkos bonkos bonkos*! Followed by *no laughs no laughs no laughs*. I stayed awake for hours with that stupid word pounding my brain! In fact, I think I had finally been driven officially *bonkos*.

Aside from that particular episode, though, *Seinfeld* never fails to lull me to sleep. (I mean that in a good way!) Joy loves it, too. Long ago, it became part of our bedtime ritual. Almost every night, we'd lie in bed watching those eleven o'clock reruns on Channel 11. Then one day, they were gone. Vanished. It turned out that Channel 11 started broadcasting the show at seven-thirty instead. So eleven o'clock would roll around and I'd lie there wondering, Where are my friends? What's Kramer up to? Who's Jerry dating? Just like that, they were gone. And, frankly, it disrupted my sleep and my life. I'm not kidding.

> *JOY: That's true. You were in a bad mood. You didn't wake up with the same happy smile.*

She's absolutely right. It really threw me off balance. So, as usual, I vented about it on *Live!* "My *Seinfeld* is gone!" Lots of viewers responded with the same suggestion: "Hey, Regis, get with it! Tape *Seinfeld* at seven-thirty and play it back at eleven."

Yeah, that's easy for *some* people to do.

But not for me. I am not ashamed to tell you that I have never mastered the VCR. I can't do it. Sorry, I just can't do it. Once in a while I can *play* something. I put the tape in, I press Play, and it comes on. (Then again, sometimes it also *doesn't* come on!) **But I cannot record.** I haven't the faintest idea how to do it.

Knowing this, Gelman—who loves to scoff at my supposed technical ineptitude—told me about a new system called TiVo that would take all the guesswork out of recording shows. Gelman is on the cutting edge, believe it or not. (He doesn't *look* like he's on the cutting edge, but believe me, he's on the cutting edge!) So he gave me this manual to read. "TiVo simplifies it all," it said. Which is good for me, because I need things to be simple.

It also said, "TiVo automatically finds your programs for you." How? "You tell TiVo what particular shows you want to watch and it will find out when they're on, what station, and record them for you automatically."

On regular VCRs, by the time you have to program in the date, the year, the time and the station—forget it! You're never going to get it done. The show would be over before I could set it. But this TiVo sounded amazing, almost too good to be true. I was visualizing how simple my life would be. I could just step right up to the screen and say, "*Seinfeld*!" DONE! On voice command! This would be the greatest thing that's ever happened on the face of the earth! "Can you believe this?" I told Gelman. "You walk up to the TV set and all you've gotta say is the name of the show!"

But Gelman wasn't so sure. "You know, I don't think so."

Long story short, we bought TiVo.

Then I left the house while Joy figured it out.

Gelman came over, too. He wanted to see our new wonder gadget. Later on, Joy tried to explain it to me. Something about a hard disk something and a download something. I didn't quite get all of it. But apparently you don't yell at the screen like I'd thought. As much as I hate to admit it, Gelman was right. You have to press some button and scroll down and there's a menu and—to quote from my favorite program— *yadda yadda yadda*. Joy studied the manual and right away she programmed in *Seinfeld*. I still got a little bit nervous about it.

That night, Gelman called me at quarter to eleven, like he always does, every night, year after year.

"Did you get it recorded?" he asked.

I told him, "It isn't on yet, Gelman! It comes on at eleven!"

JOY: It was taped, *Regis! We could have turned it on earlier!*

But I don't want to watch *Seinfeld* until eleven, all right? Can I have things my way for a change?

Anyway, I'm waiting and I'm waiting and I'm tired and I'm still waiting and finally, at eleven o'clock, I go for it and see some stirring on the TV set. My God, I can't believe it! TiVo's going to work! A picture comes into focus and guess what? It's *WHEEL OF FORTUNE* WITH PAT SAJAK! She programmed in *Seinfeld*, we got Sajak! How can that happen? **HOW CAN THAT HAPPEN?!**

JOY: I did it right. I stand by what I did. I did it correctly, and the only thing that I can think of is that they have to download your particular cable system into your TV and, somehow or other, I got the wrong channel.

Not sure what all that means, either. Actually, I have a vague idea. It means, NO SLEEP FOR REGIS. That's what it means! Why couldn't I just go up to the TV like I want to and yell, "*SEINFELD!!!*"

I AM NOT A SEINFELD STALKER!

Thankfully, Joy mastered the TiVo and, through devoted viewing, we've now become a couple of true *Seinfeld* scholars. We know everything about the cast, we know all the supporting characters, the plot lines, odd pieces of dialogue. We got a chance to prove our mastery one night not long ago when Jerry and Jessica Seinfeld invited us to the opening of the new planetarium at the Museum of Natural History. My mother used to take me there many years ago when it was known as the Hayden Planetarium. But now it's been razed and rebuilt into a spectacular state-of-the-art facility. You watch an amazing digitally enhanced film that's projected onto the enormous curved ceiling—and suddenly you're out in the farthest reaches of space. It just demonstrates what an infinitessimal speck we are in the whole panorama of things.

JOY: No one up there cares about the Millionaire.

Exactly. Nobody cares!

Anyway, the Seinfelds stopped by to see our place before we went to the planetarium. They were remodeling their apartment at the time and wanted to see how we'd redone ours. Right away, I brought Jerry into our bedroom to show him the new TiVo system. I clicked on the programming screen, which read: *SEINFELD SEINFELD SEINFELD SEINFELD*. He seemed very impressed. Maybe a little scared, but mostly impressed, all right?

And, of course, we spent a lot of time at dinner later talking about his show.

JOY: I think we bored Jessica to tears. We were really kind of moronic about it.

But when are you going to get Jerry Seinfeld alone?

Anyway, he seemed to be receptive. He liked reminiscing. Every time he said something, it would remind me of an episode. At one point, he said "bookstore." And I immediately launched into another

Seinfeld recollection: "Remember the time Uncle Leo got caught shoplifting at Barnes and Noble, and how you tried to counsel him? You took him to the coffee shop and you said, 'Leo, Leo, you can't shoplift! You're going to get caught.' And Leo said, 'Jerry. Jerry. When they catch me, I just say I'm OLD! I'm an old man! I don't know where I am! Take me home!'"

All right, maybe Jerry's eyes started to glaze over during that one. But, for the most part, he had to be flattered—at least I hope he was.

Please Don't MAKE ME SKI!

C an I make myself any more clear? I am convinced *more than ever* that there is no greater agony in the world than the agony withstood by people who love to ski. I don't understand these people! From the time you leave your house until the time you get to the top of that mountain, it's a *torturous* ordeal from beginning to end. Nothing is worth it. But skiers swear they love it. What do they know that I don't know? I don't get it at all. But there they are—out there glistening and carefree. They're schussing, they're skiing, they're happy, they're laughing their heads off. And they can't wait to tell you how great it is.

But let me tell you something: **It's not for me!** I firmly believe that if you don't learn to ski when you're a kid, you're never going to get it. Well, I didn't and I don't. What did I know about skiing when I was growing up in the Bronx? Nothing! And I liked it that way.

Here is the truth: I have been on skis five times in my life. And after each and every time, I have declared, "Never again!" But, unfortunately, Joy and J.J. are crazy about skiing. And Gelman loves it, thinks it's the greatest, and keeps trying to convert me. He keeps taking our show to snow country, keeps getting me on skis. He was there producing with his cameras when we went to Aspen where—within one hour!—**I fell off my skis and cracked three ribs**. God, the pain! Intense, piercing pain! Every turn, every breath forces you to cry out in anguish. But I tried to be a good soldier and went snowboarding and paragliding afterward for the camera, cracked ribs and all. And, once that nightmare was over, I declared, "Never again! *Never.*"

So why didn't anybody listen to me?

And why did I agree to go through it again just a few short years later? Why did we all find ourselves headed for a ski vacation on Whistler Mountain in Vancouver, British Columbia? WHY DID I SAY YES AGAIN? Let me now share the miserable details of what I promise was My Final Ski Trip Ever!

We flew to Vancouver, Canada, direct from New York—six *long* hours—and, of course, our bags were missing upon arrival. Nowhere to be found! I mounted a heroic search at the airport while everyone else stood around talking! J.J. and Joanna were laughing and scratching— nothing bothers kids on vacation. They're ready to ski—who cares about luggage? Finally, the bags were located and then Gelman decided to take us to lunch at a place called the Tea House in Vancouver's Stanley Park. He meant well but, of course, he had the wrong directions. So for the next hour and a half we were completely lost, winding and circling around this park before we found the restaurant. After lunch, it was a two-hour drive to the Whistler/Blackcomb ski resort.

By the time we arrived, it had been ten hours since we left New York. And that's when the winds started to howl and, all of a sudden, the chill factor plummeted. Out of nowhere, storms were blanketing the entire Pacific Northwest! Blizzards, gale-force winds—a weather disaster! In fact, it turned out to be the three worst weather days in the last seventy-five years of British Columbian history! The WORST. I'm not kidding— it's now in the record books. Every day, another storm. And every day, we hoped that this thing would blow over.

Well, forget it.

This one never blew over.

Actually, the first day—bravely, valiantly—we did manage to trek up to the mountain, anyway. We put on our ski boots—which is like putting your feet into two slabs of cement! And that's another thing I despise about skiing. Feet were not meant for this kind of squeezing and contorting and tugging and pinching and pulling! Especially not my beautiful, delicate feet. It's a painful, terrible process. As usual, it didn't seem to bother anyone else. Then came the layers of thermal vests and sweaters and parkas, making upper body movement almost impossible. Gelman, who knows everything about climates, had promised me that we'd have sunny, blissful weather on this trip. He said we'd ski in light sweaters and T-shirts. He was wrong.

Anyway, when we got up to the mountain peak that first day, it was 30 degrees below! Bitter cold icy blistering wind bearing down on us! Snow started coming down in sheets and it never stopped. A hazy mist rolled in! People huddled near the ski lifts paralyzed by the cold. **Other people were literally running for their lives,** clutching children to their chests to protect them! On the way up, I met a Canadian lady who told me that her two strapping sons—both born and raised in this cold, Arctic-like weather—could not take the temperatures at the top of that hill. Even they came down begging for mercy! What chance did I have?

The next two days were more of the same. I would have paid anyone big bucks to get us out of there. But, by the second day, even if we wanted to go outside, we couldn't. The snow kept coming. It barricaded the doors of the hotel. We couldn't even leave the hotel! It was three days of agony, three days of aggravation—and finally even Gelman had had enough.

And then we discovered that we couldn't get out.

We were scheduled to leave on Monday, but since the snow never stopped falling all weekend, we wondered about our flight back to New York. Everybody said, "Don't worry, the airport will stay open." Well, they were WRONG. Six-thirty Monday morning, we heard on the radio,

"The airport's closed. All flights are cancelled." People everywhere were making a run for it! Even Gelman and the staff disappeared. They were pouring off this mountain in desperate droves. I called it *Escape from Whistler Mountain!*

So now here I am with six bags and two kids and Joy. And I just want to GO HOME!! We managed to find a young man who drove us down the mountain in as harrowing a drive as you could imagine. It's still snowing like crazy, which is unusual for Vancouver. They're used to a light dusting in the morning which then disappears by the afternoon. But not today—there's snow all over the place!

Meanwhile, the airport is a mess. Most flights are still cancelled and nobody's flown out in two days! And, of course, a representative from Canadian Air meets us there and says, "Your flight has been cancelled." Now we're in shock, but we look on the screens and spot a flight to Toronto. Nice city. Maybe we can get a flight to New York from there. Sure enough, we manage to buy the last four scattered seats in coach class.

Look, I'm a fortunate guy. It had been a while since I'd flown coach. My contracts usually require first-class seating, which is a terrific perk. So let me tell you what I learned about coach: nine seats across, two against each window, then *five in the middle.* And my seat was *right in the middle* of those five! So I climb in there and sit all scrunched up, shoulders pinched on each side, nowhere to move. And there's a woman next to me with a cough. A *persistent* cough. And it begins to build and build once we're in the air. Then it becomes a full-blown coughing fit! *"MMGHAAAAHHHH! MMGHHAAAAHHHH!"* She's hacking right in my ear! But I'm prepared to live with it. My cracked ribs are aching. We've been through hell up on that mountain and we've *survived.* I'm on my way home!

But now:

"MMGHHAAAAAHH!!"

I will say, though, that Canadian Airlines is terrific and the food in coach isn't bad. But the seat-back trays are two inches from each other—and right on top of the person next to you. And, meanwhile, that lady next to me keeps coughing and now she's COUGHING ON MY FOOD! *"MMGHAAAAHHHH!"* Germs are flying all over. I just try to protect what I'm eating, shield it with my body, cup my hand around my plate and hope for the best. She's oblivious. Doesn't apologize. Doesn't say a *word*! Just *MMMGHHAAAAAHHH!!*

We touch down in Toronto at 9:10 P.M. The last flight to New York was 9:00 P.M. Because they'd spent an hour de-icing our wings in Vancouver, we missed our connecting flight by TEN MINUTES! And, of course, no bags. Yes, they are lost again. I can't believe it. No idea where they are. We spend the night in a Toronto hotel, get up the next morning at six o'clock to catch an early flight out—and guess what? *It's snowing in Toronto!* NO, NOT AGAIN! It's a cruel joke. Fortunately, we're able to get a 7:00 A.M. American Airlines flight that takes off in the snow and zips right into New York City, where I had never felt more safe in my life.

And let me tell you:

I never skied again. I never intend to.

That was it.

I'll listen to your ski stories. I'll be happy for you—*but I'll never do it again.*

NEVER. NEVER. NEVER.

And that's my final answer.

JUST PLANE MISERABLE

Air travel is my curse. Without question. I am meant to suffer on airplanes always. It's pathetic.

JOY: There was a New York Times Magazine *article about air travel that I thought you needed to read. When I think of all the things that have happened to you on planes, we're lucky you're still here. You've had more mishaps and flight problems than anyone I can think of. And you don't take those things very well.*

I spend a lot of time being FRUSTRATED, yes.

JOY: Well, the article said people shouldn't worry as much about airplane crashes, cancellations and bad food, because there are so many other things to be concerned about. For instance, the close quarters greatly increase your risk of contracting an infectious disease.

I got that a few times.

JOY: And the cramped seats can give you deep vein thrombosis.

Got that once, too.

JOY: They also described the psychological problems of people who fly a lot. Depression. Anxiety. Stress.

Got it. Got it. Got it.

JOY: Do you know what the leading cause of airplane deaths is, Regis?

Yes, tiny packs of raisins that are impossible to open!

JOY: No, heart attacks.

Haven't tried that one yet, amazingly enough!

To tell you the truth, I don't even know where to begin with my air travel horror stories. All I know is that my black cloud works overtime when I'm up in the skies. And the funny thing is, I'm not a white-knuckle flier. Once we're in the air, I can usually take the bumps—turbulence, high winds, heavy rains. I don't love that stuff, believe me, but I'd rather fly straight into the eye of a hurricane than sit trapped on a runway for two hours!

I hate hate hate runway delays.

And they get more frequent with every flight nowadays.

By now, I have probably spent more time cooped up in planes grounded on runways than I have up in the air. But let me tell you about one crazy ordeal that preceded a flight to Miami Beach where I was going to be a celebrity coach at the Lipton Tennis Tournament. This was an episode that got me so infuriated—SO ENRAGED—that I decided to scoop up the barf bag in front of me and, appropriately enough, make notes on it as things developed. Here, then, is the blow-by-blow account of just one idiotic example of my countless Flights From Hell:

12:30 P.M.: Plane is supposed to leave for Miami.

12:31: Announcement that plane is "overweight for wind conditions." Twenty-one people have to leave or we can't take off. Airline is offering $1,000 vouchers to fly anywhere in the world to those who will leave now. Is that Gelman I see racing down the aisle? Nope. So far, no takers. Most passengers don't want to leave. So we're just sitting here. Waiting. GOING CRAZY!

12:58: Twenty-one people get off. FINALLY! Thousand bucks or not, they don't look too happy, either.

1:15: We start the takeoff routine. Forty-five minutes late.

We hear a loud POP! Power goes off, engine winds down. This can't be good. I don't like loud POPs. Pilot gets on intercom. Who can understand what he's talking about? Not me. Something about "too much wind . . . mixing with the fuel . . . have to kill the engine." Yeah, right, whatever. Maybe I should have gotten off, too.

1:30: Ready for takeoff. Again. Captain gets on intercom— AGAIN. "We must move to another runway because the wind conditions have shifted dramatically." On board for an hour now. I want to get off. I envy those twenty-one people. I want to get off RIGHT NOW! But where? ON THE RUN-WAY? I feel like jumping out the window!

1:40: ANOTHER announcement from the captain: "Plane still too heavy." The plane is a 727. I look out the window and see other 727s taking off from both runways. They're shooting up into the sky. They're on their way! How can they weigh less? WHY CAN'T WE GO UP, TOO?!!

1:45: Captain gets on intercom (I was beginning to miss him): "We've got an idea! We're going to unload some fuel so that we can take off without asking anybody else to leave the plane." I will believe it when I see it!

1:55: Captain (who's now sounding like an old friend) proudly announces that fuel has been unloaded. We're now at appropriate weight for takeoff.

1:56: The flight attendant says, "The captain cannot move the aircraft until everybody is back in their seats." GET BACK IN YOUR SEATS, ALREADY!

1:59: Begin moving to our position on runway.

2:04: Captain announces that we should "prepare for take-off." Good sign. We're gonna go.

2:10: We speed down the runway and lift into the air. AT LAST!! A sullen round of applause in cabin. Nothing wrong with the plane, just a matter of freak wind conditions, we're told. Whatever. Don't understand the overweight thing at all. Also, whatever.

Of course, it was a horrible, bumpy flight. But—like all of my travel stories—this one doesn't end that simply and easily. Oh, no. So I get down to Miami an hour and a half late and, of course, whoever was supposed to meet me ain't there. I vaguely remember the name of the hotel where I'll be staying and figure I can get there on my own. I walk through the airport, which is jumping—five o'clock on a Friday afternoon in Miami, forget it!

Suddenly, a guy runs up to me, huffing and puffing—his name is Brian and he's been sent from the advertising agency to personally escort me to the hotel. We walk outside. I ask him, "Where's your car, Brian?"

He says it's in the garage. He tells me, "I'll go get the car and be back here in a few minutes."

I say, "Okay, fine."

So I'm waiting at the curb.

Forty-five minutes later, still no Brian.

You know where Brian was?

Brian was up at the Departures level.

And I'm at the Arrivals level.

BECAUSE I HAD JUST ARRIVED!

I finally took a cab to the hotel.

GRAY'S PAPAYA
SAVES MY LIFE

All right, that last story was pretty frustrating, but I can do better for you. Consider that one a warmup. I have far worse tales to share, believe me.

For instance, there are days when I will fly off to make appearances or do work in other cities and then fly back to New York on the same day. My schedule rarely affords me time for those sensible overnight layovers. Usually, I have to get right back and be ready to go on the air the next morning, no matter what.

Anyway, a few summers ago, I had to make one of those quickie in-and-out trips and fly to Detroit to do a commercial for OfficeMax. In case you're unfamiliar with it, OfficeMax is a company that sells office equipment like multipurpose phones, fax machines, computers—things I know nothing about. A car service picked me up in New York and, on the way out to Newark Airport, I perused the newspaper, then decided to close my eyes for a minute and grab a quick snooze. So I removed my reading glasses, set them on the seat and reminded myself, *Don't forget these.*

Finally, we arrived at the Continental terminal. I get out of the car, the car drives off, and now I realize: *no glasses!* I have to fly to Detroit with no glasses! Words are a blur without them. I'm going to sit on that plane and go crazy with nothing to read! So I dig out the number of the car company and find a pay phone. I figure, I'll give them a call, they'll radio the car to turn around and return my glasses. And I'm in luck—I just happen to have six quarters on me. Plenty for a short call from New Jersey to New York. So I put a quarter in, dial the number, and the operator comes on and says, "Three dollars and forty cents, please."

THREE DOLLARS AND FORTY CENTS!

I can call Hong Kong for three dollars and forty cents!

Who carries around three dollars and forty cents in change?

I'll tell you who—NOT ME!!

And, of course, I don't have a calling card. I don't know how to use those things and I don't want to know. So I hang up the phone, walk to my gate, get on the plane and began rifling through the seat pockets for something to read. Just the feel of paper in my hands might settle me down. A newspaper, a magazine, an airport map—*Anything!* If I hold it far enough away, I can at least look at the pictures. I'm already annoyed, but tell myself, Take it easy—it's only an hour and a half flight.

Anyway, I arrive in Detroit and shoot this commercial. I power through it and finish way ahead of schedule. I'm booked that night on the 9:15 flight out of Detroit Metro, which would put me back in New York by 11:15, 11:30. But now I can easily make the seven o'clock flight instead!

For once, things are going my way!

I get to the Detroit airport at 6:45 and learn that there are two flights that would do the job—a 6:55 to LaGuardia and a seven o'clock to Newark. But the Newark flight is delayed twenty-five minutes because of rain somewhere. So, of course, I'll take the 6:55 plane and go right to LaGuardia, which is much closer to town. I rush to the plane and it's packed. I mean, *packed*. Every seat is taken—*except* for the ones in the cockpit where the pilots are supposed to be.

That's right: WE HAVE NO PILOTS.

Our pilots have been delayed somewhere.

So we wait.

Thirty minutes later, at 7:15, we still haven't taken off. A flight attendant gets on the intercom and gives us the reason why the pilots aren't here. Not only do I not understand the reason, I don't understand ONE WORD SHE SAYS. Apparently, though, our pilots had been suddenly reassigned to another plane, but new pilots are now on the way via another plane—BUT NOW THAT PLANE HAS BEEN HELD UP. Got that? Good. Meanwhile, I'm sitting there, no glasses, nothing to read, *going crazy!*

I don't feel like drinking. I wish I did, but I'm not much of a drinker. Then it occurs to me that I haven't eaten anything all day and . . . *I'm starving*. It's dinnertime and nothing is being served! I'm thinking, *Gimme a peanut! SOMETHING! Anything.*

Nothing.

More than an hour has passed since boarding.

Finally, the new pilots waltz on with their white starched shirts and their shiny eagle pins and they announce, "Let's get this show on the road!" But the minute they back us out of the gate area and onto the runway. . .

A TORRENTIAL DOWNPOUR STARTS.

Lightning strikes!

Thunder booms!

Yes, the weather is too severe to take off.

More waiting.

We sit.

And sit.

FOR TWO AND A HALF HOURS ON THAT RUNWAY.

By this time, I'm so bored and restless that I say to the lady in the next row, "CAN YOU HOLD UP THAT NEWSPAPER A LITTLE HIGHER? LEMME SEE WHAT'S GOIN' ON IN THE WORLD!"

At 9:15, we finally take off—and, thank God, it's time for dinner service. Except, of course . . .

THERE'S NO DINNER SERVICE ON THIS FLIGHT.

Instead, the flight attendant walks down the aisles handing out little bags of peanuts and crackers.

You know, I remember when it used to be fun to travel.

But no more.

What happened to travel?

What happened to everything?

So I grab a couple of bags of peanuts. I rip them open—boom! boom! boom!—they're gone! The attendant hasn't even gotten past the row behind me, so suddenly I turn into Oliver Twist: "Please! Please, mister! Can I have some more?"

That's right—*I kissed up to the flight attendant for another bag of peanuts!*

But he took pity and gave me another bag.

Again—boom! boom! Peanuts—gone!

Still famished, but we're almost home.

I had to suck it up.

Finally, we touched down in New York and the same car that dropped me off that morning is there to pick me up. And, by God, my glasses are still on that backseat! My only consolation prize of the day. But it's too dark to read anything now, anyway. And besides, I'm dead tired.

But I'm also still famished!

So I tell the driver—"I've just been through the ride from hell! You don't even want to know. But there's only one way to make up for this. And that is to stop at Gray's Papaya Hot Dogs on Eighty-sixth Street."

By now, it's around quarter to eleven. We stop at Gray's and I run in there and tell them—"Gimme two to go, with sauerkraut and mustard, quickly and efficiently!" The guy hands them over.

I don't eat them.

I INHALE THEM!

One in each nostril!

GONE!

Anyway, I got home around a quarter after eleven. I dragged myself in the door. Joy was still up. I heard her voice coming from the bedroom.

"You must have had a good flight," she said. "You're right on time!"

UN-RAISIN-ABLE DOUBT

That last story reminded me of this one, for obvious reasons. Joy was pinch-hitting for Kathie Lee when I told the tragic tale, shortly afterward, of only one man and his inability to get into his bag of in-flight raisins:

ME: On the way back from Dayton, Ohio, I flew Continental Airlines. They have what they call a computer jet now that takes you right to these smaller cities, so you don't have to go through Chicago or any of these other big cities.

J.P.: A computer or a commuter jet?

ME: Commuter. Did I say computer?

J.P.: I think you said computer.

ME: All right, *commuter* jet!

J.P.: I was picturing you on this little laptop flying through the air.

ME: ANYWAY, everything was fine and on schedule. But when it came time for lunch—you don't expect much anymore. Please! Forget it. When the attendant said "light lunch"—I knew it was going to be a LIGHT LUNCH.

J.P.: Sometimes you're lucky if it's light.

ME: Exactly. So here's what they offered: a banana, crackers, a soft drink and a bag of raisins.

J.P.: Yummy.

ME: Well, you know I love my raisins. According to Kathie Lee, I'm apparently the only one that still wants raisins in his turkey dressing.

J.P.: You like raisins, Regis, really?

ME: I love raisins!

J.P.: That's right, you love raisins in your stuffing.

ME: Hello? Joy? You remember me? Thanksgiving? I'm there every year.

J.P.: That's right. Back when I used to cook a turkey.

ME: Anyway, I tried to open this bag of raisins. I pulled it this way. I pulled it that way. I tried to rip it open every possible way. Nothing worked. So I finally just gave up and said to the stewardess—"Oh, miss, could you please open my raisins for me?" Just humiliating. Well, she tried—AND SHE COULDN'T DO IT, EITHER!
   Finally, a guy across from me said, "Here, Regis, let me try." He pulled out a pocketknife and—after some struggle—slit it open. AND THAT IS THE ONLY WAY TO GET THESE RAISINS OPEN! So let me tell you something, Mr. Sun-Maid Raisin President—

J.P.: Can I just try it? [Joy takes a bag and instantly tears it open with her teeth] Want one? Here, have a raisin. You know, Regis, you just have to use your teeth a little bit to get it started . . .

ME: I can't believe it! I CAN'T BELIEVE IT!

J.P.: I have sharp teeth.

ME: You sure do. Tell me about it! But I'm in shock because I had a whole lecture—*people want me to lecture them!*—for the Sun-Maid Raisin President. Please! You have a wonderful product! JUST GIVE US A CHANCE TO OPEN YOUR BAGS!

J.P.: So all the way home you wanted your raisins and you couldn't have them?

ME: Yeah, thanks for destroying that whole bit. All weekend I said to myself, "Wait until I get on the air! I'm going to give those raisin people a piece of my mind!"

J.P.: I apparently just saved the entire raisin industry.

ME: Great, Joy. Thank you very much.

HOW MANY TIMES CAN A GUY GET THE SHAFT?

The only good news about this story is that it begins in South Bend, Indiana, where I had flown to attend a gala anniversary dinner for Father Theodore Hesburgh, the legendary president of Notre Dame. If I'm going to have to fly anywhere, believe me, I'd always prefer to fly to Notre Dame. And this had been a wonderful evening emceed by Lou Holtz, now head coach at South Carolina, who had returned to pay his respects. On the dais, besides me, were such friends of Father Hesburgh's as Coretta Scott King, Joan Kroc, and Ann Landers. The affair couldn't have gone better, but this was going to be another one of those quickie in-and-out trips.

I had brought along Bobby Orsillo, our prop master at *Live!*, who loves visiting Notre Dame with me. So, after the dinner, we raced out to the airfield to board the small five-seater plane that had flown us in from New York earlier that day. Not only did we have a show to do the next morning, but our fellow passengers included Coretta King, who had a speech to make on Long Island, and a New York priest who was scheduled to officiate at two funerals that morning. The plane was supposed to get us home by about 1:00 A.M.

But, of course, that wasn't going to happen.

We all got onboard, the engine started, and suddenly—

CLUNK CLUNK.

Just like that, the generator shaft broke.

Now, apparently these planes have two generator shafts—and you are allowed to fly as long as one of them is functional. And that's when we learned that the other shaft was also sheared.

In fact, WE HAD ALREADY FLOWN TO INDIANA THAT DAY WITH ONE BROKEN GENERATOR SHAFT!

(*Thanks for telling me now!*)

Because it was too late to find another plane, we were stranded for the night in South Bend. And that meant only one thing: a desperate late-night call to Gelman to tell him he better scramble to find somebody to pinch-hit for me in the morning. Bobby was able to wake him up and give him the bad news. Gelman took it well, but *insisted* that I somehow call into the show at exactly three minutes after nine. I guess he thought it would be a scream if I told our *Live!* viewers how I managed to avert death in a small plane crash and, therefore, couldn't make it to the studio. He knows how riveting I can be when sharing my lousy travel experiences. What can I say? It's a gift!

But, let me tell you, I didn't think this was such a great idea. For one thing, both Kathie Lee and I have worked with substitute cohosts long enough to know that there's always some adapting to do on the air. You've got to welcome the new person and shift around your concentration a little. And I knew that the last thing in the world Kathie Lee needed would be to have me call and break into that fresh exchange.

And for another thing, since I would be flying back to New York while the show started—

I WOULD HAVE TO MAKE THIS CALL FROM AN AIRFONE 30,000 FEET IN THE SKY!

Right away I anticipated a problem.

Anyway, Rosie O'Donnell—on less than forty minutes notice—was sweet enough to run over and open the show with Kathie Lee that morning. So now let me share with you how I held their rapt attention with my tale of woe, as it actually happened . . .

> K.L.: . . . Now, Rosie, you've heard us talk through the years about the fact that any time you travel with Regis, it's—

> R.O.: A catastrophe!

> K.L.: Please! That's putting it mildly. You remember Pigpen from *Peanuts*? Regis is like Pigpen. He's got this little black cloud hanging over him. So Gelman got a phone call about two o'clock this morning from him—something about not being able to get out of South Bend. So I thought, *Call up Rosie!* She's got nothing to do but her own show immediately afterward.

> R.O.: I thought you were kidding. . . . It was eight-twenty-three when you called. I got a full hour and a half before my show. You have no idea how bad I looked a few minutes ago. No idea.

> K.L.: What's that? Oh, I guess we have Reege on the line from the airplane. Maybe. Reege?

> ME: Yes, how are you?

> R.O.:Well, I'm pinch-hitting for you here, Regis. You leave me in a lurch. I look like crap, but I had to come in here for you. And where are you, up there eating peanuts? What are you doing?

> ME: You know, I was just kidding Gelman. I didn't feel like coming in today. So I'm across the street in bed.

> K.L.: Reege, what happened with the plane?

M.E.: They couldn't take off. They had a sheared generator shaft, so we had to spend the night in South Bend. We're in a plane right now. And we're pretty close to New York, as a matter of fact.

K.L.: Why don't you just parachute down and drop in? You've done a lot of wacky stunts on this show. What's one little parachute from a plane? Isn't it sweet of our neighbor Rosie to come on over and take over for you? What a friend. You know, I gotta tell you, Rosie, you're the first call I made. I said, "See if we can get Rosie." I know you live close by, and I know you're in town doing your own shows. Plus, I don't want to sit here with just anybody. You know what I'm saying?

R.O.: I understand.

[At this point, please notice that I have been completely FORGOTTEN! Please notice that Regis—up in his plane with his Airfone—NO LONGER EXISTS!]

K.L.: It is officially Assistants' Day today. So Taryn, my assistant—what a day she's had already. I had Taryn trying to reach you this morning.

R.O.: And Mary and Elyssa as well.

[HELLOOOOOOO? ANYBODY THERE? IT'S ME, REGIS! REMEMBER? SHEARED GENERATOR SHAFT?]

K.L.: I want to thank them all. But Rosie gets on the line and she goes, "Are you stuck? Are you really stuck?" And I said, "Well, yeah. But you do what you gotta do." And you said, "Well, I'll see what I can do." And like five minutes later, you're here.

R.O.: I said, "Hey, I'm going to be Regis. Enough of this show." So, Regis, I'd love to talk to you, but I'm very busy doing your show. Bye, Reege. Nice seeing ya.

*[NICE SEEIN' YA??? HOW ABOUT NICE KNOWING YOU'RE STILL
ALIVE AND SITTING ON THIS STUPID PHONE BEING SNUBBED!?]*

ME: Well, it sounds like you two are having a great time. I'll see you all tomorrow morn—

K.L.: Yeah, whatever, take your time coming back, Reege.

R.O.: Just remember, in the unlikely event of a water landing, your seat cushion can be used as a flotation device. Good-bye.

[CLICK, PHONE DISCONNECTS]

K.L.: And with him, anything can happen. Can I tell you? He came down to visit me in Florida a couple weeks ago and, I mean, I held my breath the whole weekend because I knew something would go wrong . . .

Yeah, well, keep laughing it up, you two! And thanks for all the sympathy. Means the world to me. Really.

HEADS OF STATE, STAY HOME!

In New York City, you never know who or what is lurking down the street and around the corner to thwart you, to frustrate you, to *screw up your night!* I'm not talking about muggers, either. Believe me, muggers are nothing compared to . . .

VISITING DIGNITARIES!

Every political dignitary and elected official in the world eventually descends on New York—whether it's to drop by the United Nations or to just catch a Broadway show. And when it happens, New York shuts down cold!

NEW YORK IS PARALYZED!

New York is NOT where you want to be.

For apparent security reasons, you can count on coming face-to-face with barricades, blockades, police horses, detours and gridlocks at every corner. For instance, not long ago, Joy and I tried to go see our friend Julie Budd perform at the Algonquin Hotel, which is on Forty-fourth Street between Fifth and Sixth avenues in Midtown. We got in the car and proceeded from the Columbus Circle area down Broadway and over onto Seventh Avenue. But when we hit Fifty-seventh Street—cops were all over the place, lights were flashing. To get around this mess, we turned right, went past Eighth Avenue, *over* to Ninth Avenue, *down* Ninth Avenue—until we got to Fifty-second Street. At which point . . .

It was over!

We were *dead in the traffic!!*

NOBODY'S MOVING!!

Green light, nothing!

Red light, stop.

Green light, nothing.

Still can't move!

The reason? Guess who decided to pop into town for a visit this time:

The President of the United States!

We turned on the car radio to find out what was happening. Turned out that everything was blocked off from Seventeenth Street to Fifty-seventh Street. *Forty blocks in the heart of the city—*

SHUT DOWN COLD!!

You can't drive!

You can't walk!

GOD FORBID YOU SHOULD TAKE A BREATH!!!!

JOY: *Do they really have to block off four major thoroughfares? When he's home in Washington, at least he's in his own house. The people in Washington, D.C., don't know what it's like to have a whole city held hostage for one man's visit.*

EXACTLY WHAT I'M TRYING TO SAY!!!! I was so furious!
Ooooh, I was so mad!

We just turned around and went home. That was it! No Julie Budd—
thank you very much, Mr. President!!

> *JOY: Do you remember when we were coming from the Daytime Emmy*
> *Awards one year and you had not gone to the men's room because you*
> *thought you'd be home in five minutes?*

Yeah, but that wasn't even the President. That was the Israeli Prime
Minister who tied up traffic. And I *really* had to go to the bathroom.

> *JOY: You never want to be in the backseat with Regis when he has to go to*
> *the men's room. It was ugly.*

Yes, it was ugly . . .

After yet another Emmy loss, Kathie Lee headed off to a party at the
Rainbow Room and let Joy and me borrow her driver, Zee, to take us
home in his sedan. And it had been a *lonnnngggg* Emmy show. To make
things worse, we actually had to get there forty minutes early to hear Dick
Clark announce, "We're getting close to air time. We're getting very close
now! Thirty-nine minutes to go!"

All right, Dick, relax! You'd think it was a live show or something.

> *JOY: It* was *a live show.*

Whatever.

Afterward, it was so crowded outside, you had to fight your way to
the car. And, believe me, I was in no condition to fight my way *anywhere!*

To be very frank with you, I suddenly needed to go to the bathroom! And I mean, BAD!

But I figured: No problem, we'll get the car and Zee will have us home in four and a half minutes. So we get into Zee's car, and I said, "Zee, the best way out of here is to take Madison up, turn left, go through the park and come back on the West Side." No problem. We get over onto Madison, go up a few blocks and run right smack into THE BIGGEST NEW YORK CITY POLICE BLOCKADE I'VE EVER SEEN IN MY LIFE! Not just with little police horses, but with hulking steel garbage trucks!

Netanyahu, then the Prime Minister of Israel, was loose on the East Side somewhere.

And suddenly we're in his blockade!

Total stoppage!

And now I'm getting nervous.

So I say, "Zee, backtrack up to Sixty-first Street and make a left." Which he does. We get up to Sixty-first Street and—*boom!*—another police blockade. Joy says, "Take a chance, roll the window down and let the cop see who you are. Maybe he'll let us through." She was right. The policemen were very nice and, because there were so many other cars behind us, they had to let everyone through.

That's one down, anyway.

So Zee starts up Sixty-first Street and turns left on Fifth Avenue with about twenty other cars in tow. They figure he knows what he is doing. But just as my hopes get up, we hit Fifty-seventh Street and waiting for us is *another monumental traffic jam!* There's no escape!

At this point, I'm shifting my legs around in that backseat.

Very, very, very, very UNCOMFORTABLE!

I know someone like Netanyahu needs security. But, I swear, if these visiting heads of state have coffee with somebody, the whole city comes to a halt until they decide to leave. His route of travel is barricaded so he can zip quickly from point A to point B.

Meanwhile, here we are dead on Fifty-seventh Street.

And I'm going crazy.

By this point, nature isn't just calling—

IT'S SCREAMING!

IT'S BELTING OUT "THE STAR-SPANGLED BANNER"!

I'm telling you, if Zee had been wearing a hat, I would have borrowed it! I would've bought him *twelve new hats!*

What am I going to do?

And, of course, all the stores are closed.

Everything's closed!

We keep inching along Fifty-seventh . . .

Then, up ahead, I see the Golden Arches.

McDonald's!

I thought of making a run for it. Or a limp for it.

But even that looked closed.

I don't want to bore you here, but I swear to God we spent a half-hour crawling up Fifty-seventh Street to Broadway. So by the time we actually get to Broadway, I tell Zee to just let us off in the mid-sixties instead of wasting time on Columbus. So he does, and we begin our short walk home—a walk that would have been *a lot shorter* if Joy's formal dress wasn't so tight! She hadn't tried it on after getting it altered. It looked great on her, but she could take only little steps. T-i-n-y l-i-t-t-l-e steps!

But I can see the canopy of our apartment in the distance, so I play the gentleman and walk alongside her, matching tiny step for tiny step, *grimacing with every step.* When we finally get to the canopy, I'm about to explode! So I say to Joy, "I'm going to make a run for it! I'll see you upstairs!"

I turn to go and now there's our neighbor Sue Wolf, walking her dog at eleven-thirty at night. All of a sudden, SHE WANTS TO TALK!

"Hi, Regis! How was your night?"

How was my night?

She doesn't wanna know!!

I give her a quick wave—"Hey, Sue, how're you doing?"

And—*vooom!*

I run to the elevator and press the button.

Repeatedly.

Where's the elevator?

I'm dancing a jig in the lobby!

I keep pressing the button.

Finally, the elevator opens, I get in, the door's closing, and suddenly I hear—"Hold the door!"

It's Joy, taking those t-i-n-y, l-i-t-t-l-e steps toward the elevator.

I'm getting nervous again just thinking about it.

She gets in, we zoom up to the apartment, I cram the keys into the lock, throw open the door and bolt to the bathroom.

I've never been so glad to see a toilet in my life.

THE TIME OF MY LIFE

You want another story about a typical New York night?

Try this one: *Time* magazine was celebrating its seventy-fifth anniversary with a gala event at Radio City Music Hall. And this was quite a party—commemorating not only the magazine but just about every newsmaker of the last century. President Clinton and Gorbachev were there. Tom Cruise got up to toast Muhammad Ali. Tom Hanks toasted John Glenn. Kevin Costner toasted Joe DiMaggio. Even Kathie Lee and Frank were there. It was truly the most amazing guest list I've ever seen.

Anyway, a long time ago, Joy and I had gone to another big function and, when we arrived, I said to her, "Do you have the tickets?" And she said, "No, do you have the tickets?" And so we made a rule in the house—from that point on, Joy would always handle the tickets. But the tickets to the *Time* party hadn't arrived until the morning of the event. My assistant, Pam, put them in my briefcase, it was a hectic day—and, yes, I forgot all about them. So that evening a car picked us up at seven. And, as we started to cruise down Broadway, the driver said, "Have you got the car pass?" (At these kinds of events, the police will block off the streets from here to Newark. You must have a car pass to get through the tangle.) So I said, "Yes, the pass is with the tickets. Do you have the tickets, Joy?"

And she said, "No, do you?"

Uh-oh.

Well, the traffic was thick as ever, but we slowly turned around, returned to our building, where I went up to the apartment, got the big packet of tickets out of my briefcase, came back down and got in the car again. As we're driving, Joy looked at the tickets and read this: "To all guests, please be advised. Traffic to Radio City Music Hall on Tuesday March third will be heavily congested. Please allow ample time to get to the Music Hall. Due to the attendance of President Clinton, all guests must arrive at the Music Hall by seven-fifteen."

At that point, she asked the driver, "What time is it?"

"Seven-twenty-nine."

Now, you can only push your luck so far with these things until one day they close the door and finally tell you: "You can't come in."

So we were sweating.

We were on edge.

Spoke not another word for the whole ride.

We turned down Fiftieth Street by Radio City and there wasn't a car in sight. Not anywhere! Everybody was already inside.

We were the last ones there.

But amazingly enough we walked right in without a problem. What was the big deal?

Anyway, we found our table assignment. And there was Joy sitting next to David Copperfield, the illusionist. Next to David Copperfield in full view of me was Claudia Schiffer—whoa! And the playwright Wendy Wasserstein was beside her.

Meanwhile, the seat next to me was still empty.

So I looked at the little place card to see who it would be.

I held it toward the candlelight and couldn't believe my eyes—

GEORGE BUSH!

Yes, the former President of the United States was going to be my dinner partner! It made perfect sense. I had played tennis with him a couple years earlier in Florida at Chrissie Evert's event. George and I had a lot of laughs together that day! I wouldn't be surprised if he didn't call somebody he knew at *Time* magazine and said, *"Put me next to that Regis!"*

What a night we would have now!

Just another couple of newsmaking guys, laughing it up together at the party of the year!

We could compare notes on Dana Carvey's impersonation of both of us!

We'd have screams!

I told Joy, "Wait'll you see who I've got sitting next to me! He's not here yet, but he's coming!"

Suddenly, there was a rustle beside me.

A guy sat down and said hello.

I couldn't believe it.

It was George Rush, the gossip columnist of the New York *Daily News.*

George's *R* looked like a *B.*

Nice guy, too.

I spent a lot of time looking at Claudia Schiffer that night.

POWERLESS AND WET AND TRULY
LOST IN YONKERS

All right, are you ready for this?

(Suddenly, I'm imitating Dana Carvey imitating me—*in print yet!* But that's just how bad this story is going to be.)

Anyway, this is not a story for the weak of heart. Everything in this story is about loss and frustration and suffering and inconvenience. Every single thing in this story goes wrong. But I'm not ashamed to share it. Because I survived it. Remember, though, that you have been warned!

Let's go back about four years to an October weekend of tumultuous weather—which not one television meteorologist came close to predicting. It was the weekend when that notorious Nor'easter pummeled the New York area. Nobody foresaw the intensity, the enormity, the magnitude of the storms that would hit. In fact, as a consequence, I wanted to begin a crusade right afterward to have every weathercaster in New York City fired! They did not do their jobs. Then again, if I had been properly warned, I wouldn't have this story to tell—

WHICH WOULD HAVE BEEN FINE WITH ME!

So they said there would be a little rain over the weekend. A little rain? Big deal. Who cares? That Friday we left the city and headed to Connecticut where it's beautiful in the autumn, rain or no rain. Plus there was only one thing I was really looking forward to doing that weekend— and that was to just watch Notre Dame play Air Force Saturday afternoon on television. For me, that's all I want on my Saturdays in the fall—to be left alone with my Notre Dame game. From two-thirty to five-thirty, **please don't bother me**. I'll do what you want in the morning, I'll do what you want in the evening—but please give me my sacred afternoon with the Irish!

Of course, rain had been pouring throughout Saturday morning. But by midday, the winds had begun to swirl and to gust and to really . . .

HOWL!

Do you follow me? Now, historically, if strong winds blow in Connecticut, something always goes haywire. *But these weren't just your everyday strong winds.* . . . These felt like monsoon winds! Water was now slamming down from the heavens, pounding the earth, toppling trees, flooding roads, wreaking havoc on power lines. Meanwhile, everything out in the backcountry of Greenwich where we live is connected to those power lines—electricity, heat, water, telephone, plumbing, you name it. But the most important thing connected to those power lines that day was *my Notre Dame game!*

Which was now *gone*—just like that. Along with everything else in the house.

Everything.

We had lost all modern conveniences—including the ability to flush toilets, all right? So Joy thought it might be a good time for us to leave the house and . . . GO SHOPPING! I kid you not. She had something she wanted to exchange at a store in downtown Greenwich. And, frankly, I didn't care, because I could at least *listen* to the Notre Dame game on the car radio. So I stayed in the car while she did what she had to do and while the rain poured and the winds whipped. Then, hoping that Tom and Elaine Battista might have their electricity, we drove over to their house nearby. But, of course, no power there, either. We all killed time playing cards while I listened to the game on their portable radio.

By about five that afternoon—with the rain and winds still beating—I resigned myself to the hopelessness of it all: "This power ain't gonna come back!" The only solution was to just get out of Connecticut and return to the city, but fast. So we headed back over to close down our house—*where nothing was functioning anyway.* And, on the way, I was hearing the closing moments of the fourth quarter, which suddenly had Notre Dame and Air Force locked in a 17–17 tie. The clock runs out and now there would be a dramatic overtime. And I'm thinking, "I can't do anything now. I've got to listen to this game!"

Joy goes inside the house and starts packing up. But I can't leave the car. Because I CANNOT BE BOTHERED BETWEEN TWO-THIRTY AND FIVE-THIRTY ON SATURDAY! It's my time! So I'm going crazy in the car by myself and the rain is pouring down and I'm dying with the Irish going into overtime.

Notre Dame wins the toss. I figure: *Okay, we're going to drive right down that field and smash 'em over!* We've got the ball on around the fifty-yard line . . . then Air Force jars the ball loose, recovers the fumble, then there's a penalty, then there's this, then there's that . . . then before you know it, they're down on the seventeen-yard line, they kick a field goal—and Notre Dame loses.

And it's still raining.

And I'm *devastated!!*

I'm furious!

All alone inside my car, sulking.

Meanwhile, it's six o'clock, Joy has finished packing up—and bitter loss or not, it's time to make a run for it back to New York. We get down to the Hutchinson River Parkway—and, of course, it's flooded. There's a long line of cars. Then I look over and see a tree—THAT'S RIGHT, A TREE—*floating down the parkway and heading directly at us!* **Is this tree gonna hit me!?** It just misses and crashes into a barricade between the two lanes! What next? All of a sudden, we're rafting the rapids out here!

Meanwhile, the trip to the city usually takes about forty-five minutes. But an hour has gone by and we're still on the Hutch. Finally, we're diverted onto the backstreets where all these little towns converge. And, as we're driving in circles, I realize that we're somewhere in Yonkers. In fact, yes, that's right—just like the Neil Simon play—WE ARE LEGITI-MATELY LOST IN YONKERS!

Nothing else to do but ask for directions.

I pull over to a little deli and ask the counterman how to get back to New York. This guy looks at me and says, "You know the Bronx River Parkway's washed out."

And I say, "Yeah, I know."

"The Saw Mill, also washed out."

"Yeah, I know."

So he says, "Well, what you gotta do is this—you make a left here, you make a right there . . ." I get back in the car and, of course, Joy asks, "What did he say, what did he say?"

And I tell her, "DON'T WORRY ABOUT IT—I'LL TAKE CARE OF IT!!" But, to tell you the truth, all I can think about at this moment is a Notre Dame touchdown pass that was called back earlier by a ref . . . and *I'm furious at that ref!* I can't stop thinking about that ref! And, meanwhile, I'm also trying to remember, "Under the overpass . . . make a left . . . find Central Avenue?"

All right, I completely forgot what that guy told me!

Anyway, I stop at a Staples office supply store and figure somebody here will know how to find New York. So a guy tells me, "You get on the Sprain Parkway."

"Are you sure?"

"Absolutely."

So I get on the Sprain and, by God, it is open! But, all of a sudden, there are a million red lights . . . it's slowing to a stop . . . and then it's stopped. We're diverted—and once again we're in Yonkers! *NOOOO!!* PLEASE, GOD, *NOOOO. Frankly, I don't know where we are.* But I keep going and going and finally I see Gun Hill Road—which means I'm back in the Bronx! I know my Bronx! So I head toward the Henry Hudson Parkway—also washed out—and, all of a sudden, we see Broadway. *Could this be the Broadway I know?* Of course it is! Never mind that we're at 250th Street and Broadway—what else can we do but just take Broadway all the way home!

After all, home is now straight ahead and ONLY ONE HUNDRED EIGHTY-THREE BLOCKS AWAY!

With the rain still pounding.

And with a stoplight at every single corner!

Now, New York City traffic lights are strategically timed so you can make three blocks at a time—if you ROAR OUT AND GO AS FAST AS YOU CAN before you brake for another red light. If you walk *backwards*, you can make eight blocks in the same time! But in your car you can make three.

So we crawled—block . . . by . . . block—into the 100s. Joy is hungry. I'm still furious about Notre Dame. The rain is coming down in sheets. My car is being splattered with drops as big as fists. And there are *a lot* of cars out on Broadway. A lot of traffic. It's New York—who cares about a little monsoon?

But there are no pedestrians in sight—anywhere! Where are all the people? Have they all floated away? Then, we get down into the eighties and finally we spot a couple crossing the street in front of us. Somehow the woman sees me behind the windshield. Now, normally, I don't care but I hadn't seen a human being for hours!

I was in the mood to be recognized!

I needed a little positive affirmation that I was still alive!

I see her pointing to me and telling this guy, "It's Regis . . ." And the guy is looking all around. "Where? Where? Where's Regis?"

I wanted this guy to see me!

So I'm knocking on the windshield!

"I'm here. Look at me! LOOK AT ME!!"

Finally, he sees me. And he clearly thinks I've lost my mind.

And he was right.

He was completely right.

Anyway, the trip took three hours and forty-two minutes.

We could have flown to Wyoming faster.

I started gunning for weathermen on Monday morning.

IT'S A JAGUAR, WHAT'S THE PROBLEM?

Listen to me: It's not my fault that cars betray me.

Certain people think Regis is mechanically inept. They think Regis is pressing his luck every time he takes the wheel of a car. In fact, they think Regis should never get behind the wheel of a car at all. They are wrong!

I don't cause automotive problems. I only expect performance and dependability. That's all I ask. So I have to blame the automobiles. They fight back. They always have.

For instance, my very first car was an old 1948 Hudson convertible. I bought it used in California where I was stationed on the amphibious naval base at Coronado Island, across the bay from San Diego. This was during the 1950s when the Southern California air was still clean and pure. I loved to put that convertible top down and soak up those glistening sun rays. Nothing felt better. The only trouble was that you had to take a ferry from Coronado to San Diego. (In those days, there was no connecting bridge like there is today.) And I swear to you—that car would always work fine until the moment I drove it onto the ferry. Without fail, during the seven minutes it took to get across the bay, something inside of that machine would rebel. After most ferry rides, it refused to start up again! Over the year and a half I was stationed out there, my car and I became the scourge of those deck hands on the ferry. Because they'd always have to push us off! I tell you, they dreaded—no, HATED—the sight of me and my 1948 Hudson pulling up to that ferry dock. When they saw me coming, their shoulders sank and their eyes looked away.

I'm sure it gave me a complex, all right?

Anyway, that's where all of my car problems began. And then over the years I had my share of prima donna cars, which included a used

Mercedes that just drove me crazy—some days it would start, some days it wouldn't.

But when we moved from Los Angeles back to New York, we took our time in finding the right car for our new lifestyle. After all, driving is something New Yorkers only do on weekends when fleeing the concrete crush of Manhattan traffic for greener getaway destinations. Once we bought our house in Greenwich, it made sense to get a car that suited simple, quiet suburban needs. Something solid and reliable for that weekend trek back and forth. Something ruggedly constructed and roomy enough to schlep groceries or plants and flowers. Something sedate and family-oriented.

All right, maybe we should have bought a station wagon . . .

BUT I WANTED A JAGUAR.

Everybody screamed: *Don't get it! . . . The expense of keeping a Jaguar is incredible! . . . The maintenance is high. . . . You can never get the parts. . . . If it breaks down, it can only be towed on flatbed trucks!* . . . So I was cautious about it and decided to lease a Jaguar for six months to see whether or not it might betray me. Well, nothing went wrong, so we bought it. And, let me tell you, for nine years, this car performed beautifully. I loved this car! Gray, sleek, sporty, unstoppable—it almost reminded me of me! I was never even afraid to store it in a New York City garage. (Although I could have lived without having to pay over $425 a month for that privilege!) But nothing could hurt my beautiful Jaguar! (Except maybe those parking attendants. Especially the rear fender. Ouch!)

Eventually, though, time took its toll. And then one weekend, I had a minor accident. We had gone over to our friends Tom and Elaine Battista's house and they had some people visiting from out of town. These people happened to have shown up in a **monstrous motor home**. In fact, it was the biggest motor home I've ever seen in my life and it was parked smack in their driveway! So I wedged my little Jaguar just ahead of it in the drive—no problem. But, when backing out later, I tried to circumvent the motor home and somehow I touched it with the rear of my car. Just kissed it slightly. Well, of course, it cracked a little pane of plastic right above the taillight of the Jaguar. The light still worked, but the plastic was cracked. IT WAS NOT A BIG DEAL. But Joy, of course, was outraged.

> JOY: *I thought, at least you should mention to your friends that you had just a slight little collision in their driveway in case there was some broken glass on the pavement or something. And I don't know how you couldn't see this motor home in your rearview mirror. It was quite large! As I walked out the door, Regis said to me quite sheepishly: "Um, I just hit the motor home." And I said, "Well, I think you should mention it." So finally he went inside and said, "I'm only mentioning this because Joy's making a big production out of it."*

So I hit the motor home standing in the driveway! How many people can claim that? Funny, the motor home looked better to me because I hit it!

Anyway, it wasn't a big deal! It was nothing. A few days later, when I took the Jaguar in to get my shocks fixed, I told the mechanic, "Incidentally, you might as well replace the broken taillight while you're at it." He pulled out his Jaguar parts catalogue and said, "Lemme look it up first." Suddenly, I heard voices in my head from years earlier warning me about the cost of maintaining a Jaguar.

So how much do you think that little sliver of plastic pane cost? Probably not worth more than a buck and a half, right?

A hundred and thirty-four dollars!

> JOY: *If I had been the one who hit that motor home . . .*

That's right, she never would have HEARD THE END OF IT!

Anyway, I don't even know how much the new shock absorbers cost. I was afraid to ask. All I know is that it took this guy longer to add up my bill than it did to change the oil.

AND THEN I HIT A DEER

Just so you know, I'm still shook up every time I think about this. It was a Saturday night in Connecticut and we were on our way to a little surprise party for Jack Paar, who had just recovered from surgery. Some friends were gathering at a restaurant called La Crémaillère just over the state line in Banksville, New York. So Joy and I were in the Jaguar driving from our home to the party, going no more than thirty miles per hour.

And suddenly, I saw a deer on the side of the road. He was kind of loafing along next to a wall. I felt sure he was going to jump over that wall when he spotted my car approaching.

Because Joy—for some reason—doesn't have a lot of faith in my driving, she said, "Slow down. Watch out for that deer."

I said, "I see him. I see him. He's going over the wall."

Well, of course, he doesn't go over the wall. He turns and runs directly in front of the car. I hit the brakes! I turn the wheels! But I still heard that sickening thump from hitting him! I couldn't believe it.

I was so mad at that deer.

But, thank God, I didn't kill him.

So we stopped and saw him begin to spin around in a daze. The deer clearly didn't know what hit him.

We felt sick.

Now he's spinning around and around. He can't seem to get his bearings. Finally, he lies down on the road in the opposite lane, right in the path of oncoming traffic! And now we're panicked! I'm out of the car and yelling, "Deer, get up! Get up, deer!" The deer doesn't understand me. Joy, meanwhile, was saying, "Let's get to a phone and call somebody to come see if he's all right."

But then I spot a car coming toward the deer in the other lane. So I started flashing my lights to alert the driver. The car slowed down and went around the deer. The deer, meanwhile, was now groggily stirring a little bit. I was hoping he was about to get up and lope into the trees, but we still decided to rush to the restaurant and call the police to check on the deer. In the time it took to get to the restaurant, the police had already gone to the site to investigate, but the deer was gone.

Not dead—just GONE.

So I'm sure this is what happened: Obviously, the deer got up and walked into the woods and lived happily ever after! In fact, that deer is probably eating the rest of my flower beds right now.

THE EVIL GAS CAP

I was sorry to see it go, but after ten good years, we traded in the old Jaguar for a beautiful brand-new model. Now, have I ever explained to you how much I hate change? Well, I hate change. With *all my heart*. Hate it. And, as it turned out, Jaguar technology changed a great deal in those ten years. New gauges, new readouts, new panel features, even *computers* (God help me!)—it's all very complex. So *unnecessarily* complicated! But one especially horrible new development in the Jaguar has turned the formerly simple act of filling it with gasoline into . . . AN UNENDING NIGHTMARE.

I refer to the gas cap.

I hate this car's gas cap.

This gas cap was designed to keep you from filling the car with gas! There is no other explanation for it. This cap has foiled me from the beginning. This cap has even caused marital disagreements! You want a story? Just one embarrassing story? Well, I'm not telling it alone!

> JOY: *Oh, I have to tell you what Regis did. We were on our way to Connecticut one weekend when he looked at the panel lights and said, "Uh-oh, we need to get gas." So we pulled into a gas station and he*

got out and went to the pump. Then I began to hear this grumbling back there. So I turned to see him fighting with the rear end of the car. He was twisting and banging at it and said, "I can't get the cap off! The cap won't budge!"

That's right. The stupid cap. I don't know why it does this, all right? But the cap seems to get locked.

JOY: It is funny because if you lock this car with your key, the gas cap locks automatically. I guess that's helpful to people who are afraid that somebody might try to steal their gas. So I suggested, "Why don't you go inside and ask the attendant if he knows how to open the gas cap?" Regis said, "I'm not going to do that. He'll tell all his friends that stupid Regis doesn't know how to open his gas cap. He'll mock me!"

I don't need that.

JOY: You said, "They'll laugh!" I said, "No, it's a perfectly normal request—for us." So, instead, I walked in and I saw this guy who seemed to be the attendant. And I asked him, "Do you know how to get the gas cap off of a Jaguar?" And he looked at me. And he looked at everyone around him. And he looked at the woman in a cage working the cash register—

And you guessed it.

JOY: He did not speak English. He had no idea what I was talking about.

Even if he did speak English, he still wouldn't know what you were talking about!

JOY: And the cashier lady laughed and said, "Oh, I know who you are! What's the problem?" I told her and she laughed a little more—so you were right. I got laughed at.

Yes! You got mocked. Well, I don't want to be mocked. I'm tired of being mocked. I'd rather just stand there without any gas. **YOU'RE NOT GONNA MOCK ME!** Do you understand?

JOY: So we did what we should have done from the start—we got out the dreaded owner's manual and we read.

Which is really ridiculous.

JOY: When the automatic gas cap is stuck, you have to open the trunk, take everything out of the trunk, put your hand down through the inner lining and up to release the lock.

You'd think that for fifty grand they could make it a little easier. . . .

JOY: Especially for a guy like you.

Thank you.

I JUST *TOUCHED THE CURB*, ALL RIGHT?

Those are the times when I miss my old Jaguar most. I have to say that this new model requires constant vigilance! It's like a delicate flower. For upkeep, it needs gentle care and feeding and nurturing. As a result, I have it in the shop a little more than I'd like and sometimes *a lot* more than I'd like! I'm thinking of one stupid story to illustrate this point, if you don't mind.

Let me take you back to a wintry and freezing Friday not too long ago. I had just gotten the Jaguar back from a mechanic in New York that *very* morning, in fact. It was an off-day—there haven't been a lot of those for me lately—so Joy and Joanna and I decided to get out of the city and drive up to Greenwich to do some errands. (Usually a lot less stressful when you're not fighting New York traffic.) Anyway, I wanted to get a haircut up there and the girls mentioned something about S-H-O-P-P-I-N-G. Fine.

So we drove to Connecticut. I got my haircut. Joanna raced off to get some things for herself. Then Joy said, "I want to go to a certain shoe store." Her beloved Grossman's, on the Avenue in downtown Greenwich. Now, this Avenue is a one-way street sloping down a hill and the shoe store was on the opposite end from where I got my haircut. So I took her around, dropped her off, and went to get the car gassed up. (Yes, I got the cap open this time!) But to circle back to the shoe store, you encounter a lot of traffic lights on Post and Putnam roads and I wanted to circumvent those lights.

So I was curling around the side streets in search of the fastest route back to that stupid shoe store. I'm driving along, swiveling my head like crazy looking for a street that will get me where I want to go, when suddenly I see the right street that cuts directly back to the Avenue. And, at the very last second, I make a hard quick turn, trying to negotiate the corner . . .

And CAN YOU EXPLAIN TO ME WHY THE CURBS ARE FOUR FEET HIGH in this part of town?!

Yes, I jumped the curb!

WHAT'S THE BIG DEAL!?

Please. Everybody's been up on a curb at some time or another. But this curb was so high that it tore into the underside of my car. I drove down off the curb and started hearing *wwwaaaaggghhhh* . . .

Just one of those terrible sounds that lets you know that you're in trouble.

You know, every time you have an accident, you think *thirty seconds ago, everything was fine.*

But now, here you are on a freezing Friday morning, in Arctic weather, and the guts have fallen out of your car and they're hanging down on the pavement and radiator coolant is pouring everywhere and Joy, meanwhile, is waiting for you at the shoe store and Joanna, meanwhile, is waiting for you to pick her up at Banana Republic—these people are waiting for me!—and I don't even know the name of the street I'm on and I'm stuck with this car whose guts are splattered all over the place and it's blocking traffic!

And I got *furious!*

So I do the only thing I can. I run to the shoe store to find Joy. I walk in there and the salesman says the worst thing I could possibly hear at that moment: "She just left."

I can't believe it. But then she spots me from across the street where she had wandered off. So I walk her back to the car and say, "I had an accident."

"You what!?"

> JOY: *No, you said, "I've had a little accident." And then I saw the car. Actually, I saw the whole front end lying on the street underneath the car. The bottle of coolant from the air conditioner—and everything else was just lying on the street. And you said, "But I just touched the curb."*

That's right. *I just touched the curb.*

But now we had to call a tow truck or something. I didn't know who to call, but then I remembered there was an Acura dealer nearby where we'd gotten a car a few years earlier. So I call my buddy Ralph, the

Acura dealer, who directed me to Bob's Towing Service. But the guy who answers the phone at Bob's is named Billy. Now, I've got enough on my mind, between Bob, Billy, Ralph—and the guts of my car hanging out!

And Billy's first question is, "Where are you?" And I can't think of the name of the street. So I'm running with Joy's cell phone down to the corner to see the name—

[DO YOU KNOW HOW AGGRAVATING THIS IS?]

I tell him where we are and just then a lady wheels up to me in the middle of the street, rolls down her window and screams—

"REGIS PHILBIN! Is that you?"

"Yes, lady, it's me."

"What're you doing here?"

"Don't ask."

And then here it comes.

She can't stop herself.

She says: *"Is that your final answer?"*

I have to admit it. I'm not ashamed. *I almost went for that lady!* I wanted to GET HER! But she quickly rolled up the window and drove away.

Finally, the guy with the flatbed tow truck comes—a tow truck that's the length of the whole block! At which point, I'm wondering if we can make this experience *any more embarrassing.* We climb into the truck while the car gets hoisted.

And I can't believe what's happening to me.

All I wanted was a haircut.

JOY: And Regis was now saying to the towing fellow, "This can't take long to fix, right? You'll just bring it to the shop and I'm sure they can push all of the stuff right back up into the car. Because I hardly touched the curb. We can just go have lunch and wait for it to be fixed—no problem, right?" He wasn't getting much response. So, to lighten the mood, he decides to make a big joke out of it. Because, of course, he's the one who caused this headache. All of a sudden, this is now supposed to be a funny little adventure.

All right, it was a little psychological ploy. Do I need her simmering and glaring at me on top of all this? No, thank you.

Anyway, we're now up in the tow-trailer with the car riding behind us and we ask the driver to take us down Greenwich Avenue in order to go find Joanna, who's been standing outside of Banana Republic for an hour, waiting for us to pull up in the Jaguar. So, instead, she sees us pull up in this flatbed trailer. Joanna looks at us like we're the stupid kids in the family! (At times like this, I wonder if she has a point.) She's shaking her head and says she doesn't believe what she's seeing.

We came to a stop and suddenly some lady is now knocking on the truck door. I look down and she's waving a piece of paper at me. "Regis, could you just sign this for me please?" I'm thinking, *The whole town of Greenwich is looking at me riding around in this tow truck. Is this what's become of my local reputation?* Okay, lady—whatever. She didn't even ask why I was in this truck! What does she care?

Anyway, we went to have lunch and, I thought, to wait for the repairs to be completed. And during lunch I gave the garage a call to find out *how soon* they'd be finished. The body shop guy just laughed. "What do you mean how soon? This car is going to be in here for at least a week. The whole front end is caved under and the grill area . . ."

I didn't want to hear any more.

We just rented another car and sped right back to the city. What a nightmare. Joy didn't speak to me for the rest of the weekend. No, I'm kidding about that.

JOY: No, actually, he isn't kidding about that.

A COMPLETELY LOST CAUSE

Believe me—I always know exactly where I'm going. It's just that sometimes I'm not quite sure how I'm going to get there. But I'm a man! And all men have built-in compasses! It's a fact. It's also a fact that Joy and I get lost frequently. Maybe a little too frequently. But, at least, I've always been open and honest about it. In fact, I've spent a lot of time over the years confessing—all right, *complaining*—about this problem on our *Live!* broadcasts, a couple examples of which I am not ashamed to share with you now . . . (And please note how a certain cohost has taken unmerciful pleasure beating my brains in over it!)

> **ME: Here's a big story in *USA Today*. It says that men are afraid to ask for directions because we feel like we're—**
>
> **K.L.: Impotent.**
>
> **ME: Why is that so much on your mind these days?**
>
> **K.L.: I have no reason to think about it. However, I'm sitting next to you, and I know it's always of some concern.**
>
> **ME: Anyway, it says we hate to check maps. We hate to make a phone call. We hate to stop and ask somebody. That's the assumption. But in real life, we really do stop to ask for directions. I know I do—because I can't depend on Joy.**
>
> **K.L.: But you only stop after you've been lost for an hour and a half!**

ALL RIGHT—enough of that, thank you! Here's part of another exchange when I recounted how Joy and I got totally lost looking for a bathroom fixture store in Norwalk, Connecticut:

ME: First of all, we stopped and made three phone calls to the store to get directions from the road.

K.L.: That should have been very helpful.

ME: How? I tell them, "We're here in Norwalk and we're at this intersection—how do we get to you?" Three times! We either got bad directions or else the employee would say, "I dunno . . ." I'm not kidding you. And, on top of that, we also stopped at three different gas stations to ask.

K.L.: Wait a minute. You're a man and you stopped three times at a gas station? That's a record. I'm proud of you.

ME: I didn't say *I* went into the gas stations. I slumped behind the wheel. Joy went into the gas stations! I hid. But, you know, the days of going into your local gas station and asking directions are OVER! The person you're asking—

K.L.: Often doesn't speak your language.

ME: Exactly! So that's three calls and three gas stations. Nothing! We also tried to stop a cop, but we almost had an accident. Cop gave me a look and I kept driving! Anyway, Joy and I didn't talk for about three days afterward. Very, very aggravating.

Anyway, we found the bathroom store—ABOUT EIGHT MONTHS LATER! (Well, it seemed like it.) Frankly, there are just too many mornings when I've told these kinds of stories. It's embarrassing! I wish this sort of thing didn't have to happen as regularly as it does. Of course, it's usually nothing more than a miserable inconvenience. Other times, however, it has caused me absolute humiliation. I'm now thinking of one of the worst stories about losing my bearings when somebody—and I mean Somebody—was waiting for me. I'm thinking of the night I got lost on my way to . . .

MY DINNER WITH JOHNNY CARSON (or, WHY I ALMOST CUT OFF MY SLAUSON!)

I still get nervous thinking about this. It's a *painful* memory. And it should have been a treasured memory, a magical wonderful evening full of laughs and camaraderie.

Should. Have. Been.

But it's my fault that it didn't turn out that way.

Let me give you a little background first: One of my first experiences with Johnny Carson—the once-and-forever King of Late Night Television, who presided for thirty elegant years as host of *The Tonight Show*—took place back in the mid-seventies. I was the host of *A.M. Los Angeles* at the time. My good friend Peter Lassally, who spent twenty-two years as producer for *The Tonight Show*, had arranged for me to do a rare interview with Johnny one afternoon as he arrived outside the NBC Burbank studio where his show was taped. So there I waited with a camera crew when Johnny pulled up in his little Corvette. We talked for a few moments, then I suggested to him, "Let's go inside and see what your first ten minutes at the office are like." Johnny was in a playful mood, so he first led me into the wardrobe room where every day he picked out the suit and tie he would wear on the show that night. That day he let me make his selection for him. I went straight for a puce jacket, then reconsidered. "No, Johnny," I said, "I don't want you in puce!" (Too bad there weren't any monochromatic combinations in those racks!)

Then we walked out onto *The Tonight Show* set, which was deserted, almost ghostly. But there was Doc's bandstand over to the left. And there was home base to the right—that famous desk and the window behind it overlooking the pretend panorama of twinkling Los Angeles lights. I asked him to show me the place where he waited to walk out through the curtains each night. He pointed out the long mirror where he took one last glance at himself before the rest of America saw him step out onstage. I asked him, "Do you still get nervous? After all these years?" He said, "Oh, yeah. Oh, yeah. It helps to be a little nervous." Then we walked out toward the star on the floor, the spot where he delivered every one of his monologues. I remember standing on that star and looking up at all of those empty seats. I felt like I was at the bottom of a Greek proscenium. Very intimidating. Then I followed him around behind his desk and sat down in his chair. I pretended that I was him for a minute. I don't think Johnny was too crazy about that. In fact, he kicked away one of the chair legs. "Don't get too comfortable," he joked. Don't worry, Johnny!

On the spring day that Johnny retired in 1992, I replayed that interview on our *Live!* show. Of course, we know now more than ever that Johnny's departure signaled an end to the classiest era in talk show history. It was a time we'll never see again. There will never be another Johnny Carson. But two years after he retired, I saw Johnny again. I was out in Los Angeles—this time without Joy—for a brief business trip. One afternoon, Peter Lassally and I dropped by Johnny's new offices in Santa Monica. And there he was, presiding over his retirement with the same casual elegance that he brought to his television career. He was a tan and relaxed Johnny—and also just as funny as ever. We chatted for a while in his beautifully decorated private suite overlooking the ocean. Then the three of us wandered out to lunch and laughed a lot—especially about Peter's new life as the executive producer of David Letterman's *Late Show* in New York. Anyway, the lunch was so enjoyable that we all decided to get together for dinner a couple nights later at Granita, Wolfgang Puck's famous Malibu place on the Pacific Coast Highway, not far from Johnny's home. The time was set for eight o'clock. Perfect. I was looking forward to it.

[DO YOU FEEL THE FOREBODING DOOM, YET?]

I have relived what happened next so often that my stomach is hurting now, all right?

So anyway, I remember leaving the Century Plaza Tower, where I was staying, just a little later than I'd wanted that night. I took Olympic Boulevard, hoping to find an on-ramp to the San Diego Freeway. But there's no ramp from Olympic Boulevard. So I took a street that runs parallel to the freeway for a long time before I found a ramp. Fine—except once I got on, I realized that I had overshot the turnoff to the Santa Monica Freeway, which heads toward the beach. I had found myself so far off track that I was now well on my way to the Los Angeles International Airport—completely the wrong direction! I felt like an idiot—after all, I had lived in this town for thirty years! Who knew if I would have the chance to dine with Johnny ever again? And now I was going to be late.

Let me remind you: *nothing is more important to me than punctuality.* The life of a broadcaster is all about punctuality.

But now streets that I had known and passed for years were just flying by. I knew I had to get off on one of them and turn around. And, of all the streets to choose, I pulled off on Slauson, where I quickly learned that there was no entrance to get back onto the freeway in the opposite direction. So suddenly, there I was trapped on Slauson—yes, indeed, the famous Slauson Cut-Off! How many times I had watched Johnny Carson doing his Tea-Time Matinee routine as the toupeed host Art Fern, giving directions to a car dealership located off the complicated Los Angeles freeway system! Art Fern would always instruct viewers to find the Slauson Cut-Off, then recommend that they get out of their cars and cut off their Slausons. He'd whack his pointer against that ridiculous map with a resounding swat. Always a huge laugh.

But I wasn't laughing now.

It was already past eight o'clock and I was still driving like mad all around the airport neighborhood. And Granita is at least thirty-five minutes away, which meant that I was going to be *seriously* late. Inexcusable! So I reached for the rental car's cell phone. Believe it or not, this was the first time I had ever tried to dial one of those things. I amazed myself by actually getting the number for Granita. Then I called the restaurant and explained to Peter that I had gotten lost. We've been friends for decades, but this time even Peter was stunned. He stressed that I get out there *as soon as possible*. So I hit that pedal and raced to Malibu—but didn't arrive there until eight forty-five!

And Johnny wasn't smiling or laughing—even as I blurted out my explanations and apologies. Not even the Slauson coincidence seemed to amuse him! Forty-five minutes late. For Johnny. I kept Johnny waiting. And I'm still wincing.

ONE BEEPING NIGHTMARE

I fear rental cars.

Rental cars lie in wait for me. They come equipped nowadays with features designed to simplify the lives of customers—all customers, that is, EXCEPT ME. I have no idea what most of these new features are supposed to do and I don't want to know. But, unfortunately, these cars have a way of making me feel like a moron.

I'm thinking of one particular car—a blue Buick town car—that came into my life during a Los Angeles trip not too long ago.

I came to hate this car.

With all my heart, I hated this car.

JOY: There's something about you and a car and a key that's just a hopeless combination to begin with.

139

Well, this one had it in for me almost from the start!

We had gone out to Los Angeles for a vacation and to spend time with J.J., who had just moved there for a writing job. Somehow we had picked up the rental car at the airport without any incident.

That was the good news, since it had one of those remote control keychains that I can never understand. You know what I mean—the kind that can now open your door and turn on your lights and honk your horn and change your oil all with the press of one little button. Ridiculously complicated. *Let me open my car door the old-fashioned way, please!*

I just want to turn my key in a lock and be done with it, all right?

But I was feeling confident out there.

I thought I'd get with it and conquer this thing.

Joy and I had gone to play tennis and, when we came back to the subterranean garage to get the car, I said, "Watch this!" I hit the button on the keychain.

All of a sudden, the horn started going:

BEEP BEEP BEEP BEEP BEEP.

Somehow, by opening the doors, the car alarm had sounded!

And in this concrete underground garage, those beeps just echo even louder and bounce off the walls! People were looking around, craning their necks to see what the problem was.

And I COULDN'T TURN THE STUPID BEEP OFF!

We got in the car and I tried hitting every button on the console! Nothing.

Just **BEEP BEEP BEEP BEEP.**

So I drove out of that garage—BEEP BEEP BEEP—and up the ramp—BEEP BEEP BEEP—and into Beverly Hills—BEEP BEEP BEEP. And it's kind of *embarrassing,* you know?

"Hey, is that you Regis?"

BEEP BEEP BEEP.

"Hey, Regis, how you doing?"

BEEP BEEP BEEP.

"Hey, Regis, is that your final beep?"

(I wished!)

Thankfully, it mysteriously stopped after about three minutes.

Three torturous minutes.

JOY: Then I left you and everything went wrong.

As if things hadn't gone wrong enough already!

I dropped Joy back at the hotel and went to pick up J.J., who was over in the Valley. Got there beepless, too—which was a relief. But as she opened the door to get in—

BEEP BEEP BEEP.

There it was again!

BEEP BEEP BEEP.

So she jumped in and I tore away—BEEP BEEP BEEP—and we got on the freeway—BEEP BEEP BEEP—and now other drivers were glaring at me with ugly twisted faces. I could see them screaming behind windshields: "STOP BLOWING YOUR HORN, YOU IDIOT!!!" I've got both hands on the wheel. I try to give them a smile and a shrug. They kept glaring. J.J., meanwhile, has scrunched down as far as she could in her seat. Yes, her father is embarrassing her again. Finally, after three miserable minutes, it stops.

We drove over to the Fox studios in Hollywood, where the guys from *Mad TV* have their offices. I was supposed to meet with them about a sketch appearance they wanted me to tape. We get there, park the car, go up to their office, do what I have to do, then J.J. and I come back down, open the door—and, yes . . .

BEEP BEEP BEEP BEEP.

Meanwhile, a crowd is pouring out from a taping of the Fox game show *Greed,* which they do on a soundstage right next to where my car is parked. Audience members are startled at first, but then quickly gather around me while the horn beeps away.

"Is that you, Regis?"

"Isn't that Regis honking his horn?"

"Why is he honking his horn? Probably trying to get attention."

(*"Yes, it's me—and, no, I don't want you to see me like this!"*)

BEEP BEEP BEEP.

I'm in the car with J.J. trying to turn this beeping off and I'M GOING CRAZY.

But now I can't even get the car started!

Then Dick Clark's son, Rac, who's on the *Greed* production team, wanders over to the car smiling and laughing—"Hey, Regis, come on over and say hello to our host, Chuck Woolery!"

I'm fighting for my life and he wants me to go fraternize with the competition! *Woolery!* Please!

"*I can't!* I've gotta get this stupid car out of here!"

Finally, the car starts and I'm driving through the crowd of people gawking and yelling at me, scattering them all over the parking lot! At least I don't have to beep the horn to get them to move!

Because the horn is beeping by itself!

BEEP BEEP BEEP BEEP.

By now I'm thinking J.J. is ready to seek adoption!

J.J.: I was laughing really hard, because when my dad does something like this—something that's actually his fault—then it becomes funny. When it's not his fault and just bad luck, he gets exasperated—and then you get a little scared. You want to run for your life. But since he was the one who couldn't figure out the alarm, he was smiling and waving at everyone.

Well, you've got to make the best of a bad situation.

Anyway, we pull up to the studio's guard shack on Van Ness Avenue and the guard says, "Hey, Regis, your alarm is on!"

No kidding.

Like I haven't noticed???

But we're out of there and the beeping finally stops again. I drop off J.J. for an appointment at the William Morris office in Beverly Hills. She gets out and, sure enough—AGAIN!!!

Every time that door opens . . .

BEEP BEEP BEEP BEEP.

I want to just jump out of this car and leave it—FOREVER!

Next stop is picking up Joy around the corner at Neiman Marcus! *There's no escape.* She had told me to meet her outside the store, so I'm driving down Wilshire Boulevard in the middle of Beverly Hills, where stylish people are staring at me and pointing and laughing their heads off—

BEEP BEEP BEEP BEEP.

And I know one thing for sure:

There's *no way* I'm going to pull up to Neiman Marcus with this thing blaring!!!!

JOY: Well, I heard you coming. I didn't want anyone to see me anywhere
near you and that car. I didn't want anyone to know. So I ran down
the alleyway and I intercepted you.

You said, "GET IN!"

And I said, "I'm not going to get in with that alarm beeping. Just
give me the keys!"

You said, "Just get in the car."

And I said, "Give me the keys, because I think I can fix it, Regis."
I took the keys, I put the key in the door, turned the lock and the beep-
ing stopped. That's all it took. You see, Regis, you'd been sticking your
arm through the window to open the door. You're not supposed to get

into a car like that after pressing the alarm button. You have to use the keys.

Maybe so.

But here's my motto forever:

NEVER PRESS ANY BUTTONS TO GET INTO A CAR!

Just use the key, stupid, and drive happily ever after.

NO MORE NEW TECHNOLOGY!

There. I said it.

And I mean it!

Maybe you've figured this out by now, but technology and I don't mix. I guess I'm what you might call a techno-klutz. *And who asked you, anyway?*

But I'm proud of it. I don't need to hear about how every new machine and gadget in the world is simple enough for a child to use. I say: Then go get a child to use them and don't bother me! Just keep your microchips away from me. They are designed to complicate and ruin my life!

Joy, however, is something of a techno-wizard. At least, compared to me she is. *And she's never been shy about pointing it out, either . . .*

> JOY: *Regis doesn't even know how to work air-conditioning. He'll say to me, "I don't know how to turn the air-conditioning on or up or down. Can you please do it!" When we leave the house in Greenwich, there's a whole series of tasks to perform—you have to set the alarm, you have to turn off the air-conditioning, you have to lock up. And these are all my duties while he sits in the car honking the horn. This is what I love about him. But, of course, one of us has to know what we're doing.*

I'll tell you where I especially don't *want* to know what I'm doing:

Joy has a desk in the corner of our bedroom that's like an amateur CIA surveillance compound. Not only does she have a computer and a fax machine there, but her phone has a built-in answering machine and features like Caller ID, Call Waiting, Call Vaporizing, Call Ionizing—I don't know what half of it means!

JOY: And you can't work any of it.

I don't want to! I just want to be able to make my calls! Is that too much to ask?

But even that turns into a major challenge.

These telephones that they make nowadays are so fragile that if you look at them cross-eyed, they break. Not like the old-fashioned models—you could run those over with a train and they'd still work fine. But this phone of Joy's is very *delicate.* One night we came home and I decided to check to see how many messages we had on the answering machine. The bedroom happened to be pitch dark—I couldn't see a thing. BECAUSE I DON'T WANT TO SCREW UP THE LIGHTS BY EVEN TOUCHING THEM! Anyway, the only way I could see what I was doing was to tilt the phone toward a light in the hallway. I could tell there were a couple of new messages and a lot of old ones that were saved. But the minute I tilted the phone, it disconnected and we lost all the messages. *Just tilted it! Gently!* And, of course, you-know-who was very upset about it. An *uncomfortable* night!

Then there's the other phone in my little office. It's plugged into an electrical socket that connects with the light switch at the doorway. But you must not turn that switch on or off—or else the phone will shut down. **I DON'T KNOW WHY—IT JUST DOES!** That's the way they built the apartment. Believe me, it was the most screwed-up system in the world. But you had to leave the switch ON at all times. And I'd told Joy this over and over and over again.

Anyway, Joy forgot. She hit the switch instead of turning off the lights by hand, and killed all the power to the phone. So for weeks it went *beep beep beep beep.* All night, every night, I could hear it! Closed the office door. Still, *beep beep beep.* Like Chinese water torture! Joy said the phone had to be "reprogrammed." I said, "Are you asking *me* to reprogram the phone?!" Anyway, she got it reprogrammed before I could throw it out the window.

> *JOY: I remember once coming home from a skiing trip to find everything in the house shut down. The fax machine was out of paper—and because Regis doesn't know how to reload it, we never got a single fax the whole time I was gone. My outgoing announcement on the answering machine had been erased because he had somehow hit that improperly. So there was no answering machine. He was living in the eighteenth century and he didn't even know it. I mean, nobody could reach him.*

And do you want to know something?
I really enjoyed the peace and quiet.

OUR ELECTRONIC CRICKET

By the way, never ever put a fax machine in your bedroom. It's a very stupid idea, but we did it anyway.

Why did we do it?

I don't know.

As bad as it is to hear a phone ring in the dead of night, there's nothing quite as chilling as the sound of a fax sputtering its way through your machine at three A.M. Whenever I've heard it, I can only think of one thing:

Joy's sister Janet has a breaking bulletin that she can't wait to share!

JOY: You know that's not true. Although it does usually happen with people faxing from earlier time zones. I remember one strange three o'clock fax that you slept through entirely. We had gone on our Alaskan cruise where I bought a beautiful parka in Sitka. They sent it to me, but there was a slight problem with it. So I faxed the man at the store and asked him if he could solve this problem, but never heard back for weeks. Then one Monday morning at three came a fax giving me my answer—which was peculiar since it would have been ten o'clock Sunday night his time.

What did he say?

JOY: That he couldn't help me. But he woke me and I never got back to sleep for the rest of the night.

You see, that's why I don't want technology anywhere near me!

Here's another reason:

Too many machines make electricity do weird things!

I remember a period of weeks when we were convinced that something—or maybe even *someone*—had infiltrated our bedroom and was hiding in the shadows. We kept hearing this strange noise all night long—

Brruuuppp.

Brruuuppp.

Whenever I tried to get close to it to see what or where it was, it went silent. Then when I'd back away again—

Brruuuppp.

I thought it had to be a cricket or maybe even a sparrow that had flown in through the window and couldn't figure out how to get back outside. And since we're more than fifty floors up, it had to be a very *ambitious* cricket! A crafty cricket.

Because I couldn't find it.

I just wanted to help it get back to its family.

I opened windows and commanded:

"FLY OUT!

"Do something!"

Nothing happened.

Just *brrruuuppp*.

All day, all night—*brrruuppp*.

For a while, I thought it was the fax machine, but every time I got near that desk—silence! Then: *Brrruuppp!*

Finally we figured out that it was the surge protector on that power strip where Joy had twelve of her CIA machines plugged in! So we had to disconnect everything—and no more *brruuppp*.

Funny part was—I liked it better when I thought it was a cricket. I kind of miss the little guy.

WHY I DESPISE CALL WAITING

I want to stamp out Call Waiting.

I HATE IT! It's the most hated thing in my life!

Honest to God, every time I pick up the phone to make a call, somebody beeps in! **It makes me very nervous.**

Every time I hear that sound, I go nuts!

First of all, when the other person is talking, it's impolite to interrupt them and say, "Please stand by, I have another call."

What does that mean to them?

That perhaps they're less important than the next caller.

Second of all, **IT DRIVES ME NUTS!**

JOY: Regis simply cannot grasp Call Waiting. He's tried, but he always loses one of the callers. I remember once he was in the midst of a very important negotiation with somebody from ABC, and our cleaning lady's daughter buzzed in looking for her mother. Well, of course, he clicked off to get the incoming call and lost the ABC person. Boy, was he steamed. Our cleaning lady's daughter has not called since.

PRESS ZERO FOR NO CELL PHONE!!!

I swear to God, I think I'm the only person in this country without a cell phone. And I *like* it that way.

These things have taken over the world! Everywhere I look, somebody's yapping away on one—in cars, in restaurants, in locker rooms, on street corners! They're really getting to be a public nuisance. They go off during Broadway plays, right in the middle of dramatic scenes. Whenever it happened during the run of *The Iceman Cometh* starring Kevin Spacey, he'd just break character and scream, "Tell 'em we're busy!"

Joy was cohosting with me one morning after *somebody's* cell phone went off during a movie screening the night before . . .

> **J.P.: Did you hear that phone ringing in the middle of the movie? I said to myself, "I hate people who bring their cellular phones to the theater."**
>
> **ME: And who was it?**
>
> **J.P.: It was Gelman.**
>
> **GELMAN: It was not. I checked my phone and it wasn't ringing.**

ME: Gelman, YOUR PHONE RANG! You picked it up and said hello! What are you talking about? I heard it myself.

G.: I pulled it out and it wasn't ringing. It was a guy next to me.

ME: Oh, please! There was a woman next to you!

J.P.: You had a conversation into a dead phone? Is that what you're saying?

G.: I wasn't talking into my phone.

ME: Gelman's a little punchy these days!

Naturally, it was Gelman who gave me my first and only cell phone a couple of years ago. He thought this would make it easier for him to track me down and bother me with questions about the next day's shows. It was a nice phone, too—an AT&T with great range. Only one problem: The zero on the keypad didn't work. You pressed *0* and nothing happened. I could receive calls, but I couldn't make any. At least, not to phone numbers with a zero in them. (You'd be surprised how many phone numbers have zeros!) So I thought, *Why don't I send it to the AT&T repair shop?* But there are no more—they're ancient history!

Now, you have to call an 800-number.

That is, IF YOUR PHONE CAN REGISTER ZEROS!!!

What a royal pain!

But I tried it—and it was a NIGHTMARE! I decided that I wanted *witnesses* to what I had to endure to report my problem. So I took the AT&T repair center 800-number to work one morning and made this call on the air:

ME (*checking the number*): Is that an oh or is that a one?

K.L.: Looks like a zero to me.

VOICE ANSWERS: Borderline Industries.

ME: Uh-oh, I'm sorry. I misdialed. I'm sorry! Excuse me! I apologize! Goodbye, lady. (*I hung up and tried again*)

K.L.: You are unbelievable.

ME: Well, it LOOKED like a zero. But I can't wait for you to hear this because this is great!

AT&T Recording: Thank you for calling Lucent Technologies Consumer Product Line.

ME: Right, I understand.

AT&T Recording: This line offers troubleshooting, operational assistance and repair support.

ME: Exactly what I need! See, I pretend it's a live voice there—it helps me to believe they actually care!

AT&T Recording: So that we may direct your call to the appropriate representative, listen to the four following options for selection. You may enter your selection at any time. For AT&T's long-distance services, press one . . .

ME: I don't need that.

AT&T Recording: If you're calling about a product for which you receive a monthly bill or if you'd like information on how to lease a product, press two . . .

ME: No, I'm not.

AT&T Recording: If you are calling about a small business system such as the Merlin, Buckner or Sprint . . .

ME: No!

AT&T Recording: For all other products, including purchase and repair information, press four.

ME: Yes! (*I pressed four*)

AT&T Recording: For information on where to purchase products or to place an order, press one. For repair information, or if you have questions about how to operate your product, press two. To check the status of a product you have already sent in for repair, press three. To purchase telephone products and accessories or to place an order, press four. To repeat these options, press six.

K.L.: PLEASE DON'T PRESS SIX!

ME: I don't know what to press! Let's try zero for an operator!

AT&T Recording: That was an invalid entry.

ME: All right, six, he said! I'm pressing six again!

AT&T Recording: Please stay on the line for the next available customer service agent. Your estimated wait time is ten minutes.

Ten minutes! I'd already been on the line for a week! But that's what it's like trying to get a phone fixed today! So let me tell you what happened the first time I made that call: The recording nonsense went on forever. The options and the things you have to press—ridiculous! Finally, a live voice came on and asked, "What's your problem?" I told him, "I can't press the O." He said, "Hang on! We're going to give you the number for our repair service." So the guy put me on hold.

AND HE NEVER CAME BACK!

And that's why I proudly remain the only person in America without a cell phone. I couldn't be happier about it.

I WON'T SURF, DON'T ASK ME

And when it comes to computers, forget it!

For the most part, I'm lost. I mean, I'm more advanced now than ever before, but that's not saying much. Until recently, for me even to press the POWER and the ON buttons—TOO MUCH!

About six years ago, I decided it was time that I entered the Computer Age once and for all. I even had a guy come over one afternoon and spend an hour and a half teaching me the basic ins and outs on my laptop model. And I kind of got into it. In fact, I was actually *liking* it. *This ain't so hard after all,* I thought.

Of course, the guy was sitting right next to me the whole time telling me what to do. We were pressing buttons and things were shooting up on that screen—and, boy, it was fun. To use a phrase I'm pretty familiar with—I was feeling *confident, strong.* Since I was now trained and ready for life on the Internet, we snapped the laptop shut and he left me to get started at my new hobby.

So that night, I thought I'd get back into the computer and fool around. You know, even do a little surfing. Well . . .

I COULDN'T EVEN GET IT OPEN!

I couldn't find the lock to lift up the screen. I pressed every inch of that thing and it wouldn't budge. It stayed shut for a long, long time afterward. I figured that's the way God wanted it.

But a few years later, I couldn't stand being left out any longer. I needed to get back ON-LINE! Everything in the world is on that Internet—pulsing, blinking, growing! There's even a *Live! With Regis & Kathie Lee* website and a *Who Wants to Be a Millionaire* website. How could I not pay attention? The Internet is the future. I wanted to be part of the future and become A FUTURE MAN!

Well, let me tell you, becoming part of the future was a lot of work! First, there was the whole ordeal of hooking everything up to the phone lines in our apartment. Now, this building that I live in happens to be a great building—except that when they put the phone system in, they really made a mess of it. Until they finally changed it not too long ago, it made both Joy and me—but especially me—CRAZY! I swear to God, I'd get so aggravated—*so annoyed*—**I wanted to punch out the wall or something!** And because you need two lines to make this Internet thing work, some rejiggering had to be done.

Frankly, it was so confusing that I had no other choice—I finally had to call Gelman over. Gelman is a true son of the computer age. When he got there, he looked everything over and said, in that superior tone of his, "Now, do you have some tape? I'll need tape." Of course we've got tape! I showed him five different kinds of tape! Sometimes he treats me like some sort of apprentice who doesn't know what's going on! Please, Gelman!

Anyway, he got down on his hands and knees and sorted out the whole mess. He really was terrific. Very patient. We worked diligently for half an hour. He put a splitter in the phone line so that half the power went to the phone and half went to the computer. Finally, he got it done, then got me on-line, made sure everything worked and left.

Now I was sitting behind the desk and, yes, I WAS ON-LINE! Finally, I'd become a bona fide computer-head, a surfer, a nerd! I even had an on-line name and my very own five-letter password, which I can't tell you. If I told you, I'd have to kill you. Go ahead, try to figure it out. You'll never crack my code! Never!

All right, it's *Reege*.

Couldn't think of anything else.

So I was looking over my computer, thinking, *Boy, this is great. I'm in the future!*

Then the phone rings.

There's a phone conveniently placed next to the computer, so I answer it.

It doesn't work!

I run all over the house trying to find one that does!

The computer works, but the phone doesn't! Not a single phone in the house! In fact, neither does anything else. Even the fax machine is dead. I think the water stopped running, too!

Thank you, Gelman!

Anyway, there were too many wires coming out of the wall—plugs, wires, triplexes! My head was swimming! I had to take a break. So I shut off the computer and closed it up.

A few hours later, I was sitting there, bored—no hobbies—staring at the computer. So once again I decided to fool around with it and get on-line with my friends.

And that's when I was reminded of why I gave up on this computer years before.

That's right . . .

I COULDN'T GET IT OPEN!

Again.

For the Love of JOY

P icture this:

I'm sitting on my veranda outside my suite on the *Crystal Symphony* cruise ship, in full view of the gleaming white city of Teramina, Sicily—nestled under awe-inspiring Mount Etna. The mountain has erupted eight times in the last century. And even on this gorgeous Sunday morning in June, I can see wisps of smoke slipping out of that hole on top. I want nothing more than to just keep staring at this natural wonder. But I won't be allowed that pleasure. No, I will be denied. And here's why: No matter how much I love cruise vacations, there's only one problem with life at sea, as far as I'm concerned—

And that's when the ship stops.

Please tell me—why do they have to stop at these various ports along the way? *Why?*

It usually means waiting in line, getting on a transport tender to the harbor, then finding a bus or a cab to the main street for . . .

Oh, God help me . . .

SHOPPING!

Yes, the *dreaded* shopping . . .

One store after another, each one of them beckoning to Joy.

She never resists their call.

Not ever.

I don't even go in them anymore—I just stand outside and wait.

Sometimes not so patiently.

I stand there as the tourists and my fellow passengers stream by. And, of course, every one of them yells at me—*"Is that your final answer?"* And: *"I want to be a millionaire!"*

So why don't I go inside?

Because I can't stand it.

Joy, you see, is a careful, *fastidious* shopper. She wants to see all of her options. She will stand there at the counter for hours, as the saleslady drags out one bauble after another. In the beginning, they are eager to wait on her. But then, slowly, they realize what I know better than anyone alive: This is no pushover. This is no inexperienced neophyte.

THIS IS A VETERAN SHOPPER WHO CANNOT AND WILL NOT BE RUSHED!

And, after she sees what she wants, there must be a Time of Reflection.

She must think about it:

What does she have back home in the closet to go with it?

Is it worth it?

Can she get it in New York?

If so, for how much?

And, all this time, I am waiting in the street outside, hoping she'll come out. *Please, God—let her come out.* I smile at the tourists, tell them: "Yes, you can be a millionaire!" And: "For God's sake, that is my final answer!"

Why, oh, why, do these cruise ships have to stop?

Why can't we just keep going and never stop?

JOY: That's all very nice, but the truth is that Regis sits outside all of those stores and usually takes catnaps. And I believe the real reason he doesn't want to go into a store with me is very simple and calculated: He knows that I know that he's sitting around outside, counting the seconds. If you had somebody sitting out there waiting or falling asleep in public, wouldn't you hurry up?

Another store, another nap. It's the only way I can survive it!

JOY: But you know that I like to bring back some little memento from wherever we travel.

I remember the last time we were in Europe and you found a beautifully woven doormat in Amsterdam *that you had to have.* You went on and on about how it looked *sooooo* Dutch—which I thought was hysterical. So we bought the doormat and I took it on *Live!* to show it off. And while I was holding it up to the camera, I noticed a little tag on the back that said *MADE IN LOUISIANA!* We had a ball with that one!

JOY: I took off the tag afterward. These things have to be made somewhere. Why not Louisiana?

Joy thought it was an authentic local artifact!

JOY: Well, did you think I should have brought home something more expensive?

No, but it would be nice if YOU DIDN'T BRING ANYTHING HOME AT ALL!

GIVING TILL IT HURTS

Here is the truth about wives—mine and everyone else's. Those special occasions come along—birthdays, anniversaries, Valentine's Day, even Mother's Day—and you want to give her something meaningful, something that she wants but maybe doesn't want to buy for herself. So you ask her what she would like. You ask what would make her happier than anything else. And she will give a big sigh and tell you, "*Ohhhh*, I don't need anything . . . Just a lovely day with my family would be more than enough . . ."

Listen to me:

DO NOT BELIEVE HER!

Under no circumstances believe that she means this!

If you come up empty-handed, I promise that you will hear:

"Where's mine? Where is it?"

In your defense, you will repeat that she told you she didn't want anything. Let me tell you now: THIS DOESN'T WORK!

"Well, all I meant was that I didn't want anything *big* or *extravagant* . . . But *something* would have been nice!"

And that's when you know that you had better go find something *big and extravagant and buy it as soon as possible!* Whatever the cost, you will pay a steeper price if you don't.

Now, Joy likes baubles.

She knows as much about them as practically any professional jeweler in the business. Even our friend Lawrence Krashes—an executive at Harry Winston—is intimidated by her. He has sold jewelry to the savviest customers all over the world. But he will state, unequivocally, that Joy is the toughest, most unpredictable shopper he's ever known. One time he urged me to buy a certain piece for her—he was convinced with all his heart that she would love it. She returned it a few days later. Lawrence has never gotten over it, either.

Nevertheless, I won't even try to buy anything for her unless Lawrence—or somebody, *anybody!*—is guiding me. I WON'T GO ALONE! I'm just not that secure. I learned my lesson the hard way.

Let me take you back about twenty-five years, back when I used to be very confident about my purchases. I came home with a gift for her— one that I'd selected very carefully, mind you. I don't remember the occasion. But I do remember Joy sitting at the dining room table with her sister Janet, whom I used to call The Winds of War. I made my presentation right there, so The Winds could eat her heart out. Tentatively, Joy opened the package. And there they were—a gorgeous pair of earrings.

Joy smiled.

The Winds remained expressionless.

I expected that.

But then she began smiling, too.

But it was a certain smile that I have only come to know after I have committed a faux pas.

My blood began to run cold.

Beads of sweat formed on my brow.

What could it be? What had I done now? Yes, The Winds smiled broadly, as if to say, "Look what you've done now, you jerk!" There was silence.

Then Joy patiently explained, "These earrings are for *pierced* ears. I don't have pierced ears."

How could I not know that?

How had that escaped me?

That was the turning point. My confidence faded completely at that moment. Even now, all these years later, I remember it like a knife in my heart. I've never gone shopping alone again.

MY TWO CENTS' WORTH

But just to show you that even the most discerning eye can be fooled—ONCE!—let me tell you this story:

After living for so many years in California, we had moved to New York and been there for no more than a month. Joy and I were walking along Madison Avenue when, all of a sudden, a guy came up to me—*pssssssst*—with a bracelet. Maybe it was hot merchandise—I didn't know. But, boy, this thing was gleaming. He held it there in the afternoon sun and I was knocked out. And, yes, so was Joy. She gave me a look that meant: "Ask him how much?" So I did and he said four hundred bucks.

I thought, *Hey, I didn't fall off a turnip truck! I was brought up in the Bronx, I know my way around!*

I said to this guy, "I'll give you $200."

"You gotta deal!"

So I handed over the $200 and took the bracelet.

Now, both Joy and I walked away absolutely convinced that this guy had no idea what he was selling. This beautiful bracelet, she figured, must be worth plenty. What a buy we'd gotten!

So the next day we took it to Lawrence Krashes at Harry Winston, who was going to tell us about the thousands and thousands of dollars this thing was really worth.

He took one look at it and said, "This is worth two cents."

I said, "It's not worth two cents! You're crazy! YOU'RE WRONG. Take it upstairs to your guy with the monocle!"

He took it upstairs, then came back down, and repeated, "This is worth two cents."

I said, "Take me to the guy with the monocle!"

So I went upstairs MYSELF, but not to the same guy he went to. I went to another monocle guy. This one took the bracelet, put it under his glass, chuckled and said, "Two cents."

That's what it was worth.

Joy never wore it after that.

But, occasionally, I'll put it on.

Two cents, but it looks beautiful in the sun.

WAR AND BREEZE

This is what it has come to. One morning on *Live!*, Joy made this shocking announcement:

J.P.: Okay, Regis. I've been saving this for the show. I wanted to make this a public announcement on the air, because I thought this was the safest place. My sister Janet is coming to visit next week. And, in case Janet's watching—don't take this personally, Janet. It's just that we've had sort of a continuous stream of visitors lately, I wanted to break it to Regis gently.

ME: Janet's coming, huh? She is formally known as THE WINDS OF WAR, but I'm not supposed to call her that anymore.

J.P.: I just didn't know when would be a good time to tell you.

ME: Well, this is NOT a good time! This RUINS the whole show! When is she coming?

J.P.: That would be on Sunday.

ME: Sunday. And how long is she staying?

J.P.: A week. That's a reasonable amount of time.

ME: It is for her. I love having your family here to join us, Joy. No, a week—that's fine. Not a problem. Did you get that in writing?

Let me tell you something: When you marry a woman, you're not only marrying her—you are marrying her family. Her entire family. Make no mistake about it. Now, Joy has two sisters—Janet and Marilyn—and, over the years, they have made many, many trips to come visit us in New York. Sometimes they came separately, sometimes they came together, sometimes one might bring her daughter—and always they have brought luggage. Hulking bags of luggage that you have to continually step over to get anywhere in the apartment. And that's fine. I understood. They would shop and fill those bags and go home happy.

Eventually.

But there's something about sisters. Sisters are so close—and these three Senese women are no exception. You marry a woman, you live together for a long time, you think you're close, you think you know everything about each other. And then the sister comes in and you realize how close they actually are—and how YOU'RE not! The routine usually works like this: Janet or Marilyn will arrive and we'll stay home for dinner that night. And then the sisters start talking at the dinner table. And they keep talking and laughing and mentioning things I've never heard before.

And what I will do is this: Very slowly, very quietly, I get up. I pick up all the empty plates and go into the kitchen.

AND I NEVER COME BACK!

They don't notice anyway.

JOY: But after many, many years, you've finally realized that they weren't going to move in with us.

You're right. That was a key moment for me. All men have that fear and have to get over it.

But your sisters know I'm very fond of them. That's why I can kid them and even gave them their nicknames: The Gentle Breeze and The Winds of War. I gave Marilyn, the youngest sister, The Gentle Breeze, which tells you a little bit about her personality.

> *JOY: Now that's not a fair name, Regis. She just happens to be very sweet and a little more mellow than Janet.*

A *little* more mellow?

> *JOY: Just a little more.*

Well, you and Janet are definitely on the hyper side.

> *JOY: We're more alike, yes.*

Marilyn, though, is sweet, as you say, and thoughtful.

> *JOY: Appreciative.*

Quiet, appreciative.

> *JOY: Undemanding.*

Undemanding but never rouse an undemanding Senese sister. She'll never be the same.

No, I'm kidding! Marilyn comes to town with lists of things she wants to see—museums, art exhibits, Broadway shows, television tapings.

> *JOY: Whereas when Janet comes, there are only three sights she wants to take in—and that's Bloomingdale's, Bendel's and Bergdorf.*

But The Gentle Breeze has a nice effect on you. You two go out and visit more worthwhile sights. You've said she was always the more cultured of the three sisters.

> JOY: I remember one time Marilyn came to a Live! broadcast and sat in the audience. You did a whole number on her and talked all about her being known as The Gentle Breeze. That night, you were out of town, so she and I went out to dinner before going to the theater. We were sitting in the restaurant, talking back and forth—some of it kind of private and personal. I've gotten used to the fact that people sometimes recognize me from the show, so you never know who's listening. But this time, it was Marilyn who got recognized. A guy came up to the table, leaned over and said, "You're The Gentle Breeze, aren't you? You know what—you'll never make it in New York. You can't be gentle in New York!" See what kind of a reputation you've given her?

You should have brought him home to meet Janet! SHE'LL MAKE IT IN NEW YORK! SHE'LL MAKE IT ANYWHERE!

LATE AND LATER

There are such tremendous differences between men and women, it's a wonder any marriage survives today. Of course, if you don't have that difference, then you don't have anything. I'll tell you, though, there's one thing about Joy that drives me nuts—and I don't mind revealing this, because it's been the source of many arguments over the years.

IT'S HER INABILITY TO BE ON TIME!

I'm a broadcaster. My whole life is about being on time. Being on time is *essential*. This clock isn't gonna wait! You've got to be there.

To me, it really is a sin to be late.
I can't help it.
And Joy can't help being late.
The examples are boundless.
It happens all the time.
How about this one:

There was an evening we were supposed to meet Gelman and Laurie at a screening of the John Travolta-Nicolas Cage movie *Face/Off*. That night Gelman got a little sample of what has aggravated me for all these years: Joy's tardiness.

> *JOY: Well, the last time I had rushed to get to one of those screenings, we ended up waiting forty minutes. So I figured there was no hurry.*

Just because one movie doesn't start on time doesn't necessarily mean the others won't. And I was angry about that myself, waiting forty minutes. But some of these things actually start on time. So if the invitation says seven o'clock, you should be there at seven o'clock.

> *JOY: I was out all day. I had a lot to do, and I didn't get home until five-thirty. And by the way, the screening started at six, not seven.*

Anyhow, Gelman wanted us to meet there early because the whole movie is based on the initial five minutes. If you don't see that, you're dead. So he said, "Why don't we leave at twenty to six?" Well, I knew that would be impossible. Then he wanted to leave at a quarter till six. Again, impossible. I swear, sometimes it feels like I'm torn between two lovers! I don't know what to do! I'm trying to keep her happy and Gelman was saying, "Let's leave early."
Like the song says, it's two different worlds!
I CAN'T HANDLE IT!

So I made a compromise and Gelman bought it. Ten to six, we'd leave our apartment, jump in the cab, and we'd be at the theater by six. It would probably start twenty minutes late. But we'd be in our seats by then, no problem.

At ten to six, Joy still isn't ready.

THE WORST!

And I'm waiting at the elevator down the hall.

And, as I do almost every night, I'm yelling—

"JOY! JOY! THE ELEVATOR'S COMING!"

And these poor people who live on our floor are probably looking at each other in their apartments, saying, "Is she late *again*?"

At about six minutes to six, Joy's finally ready. And that was really pressing it for her. We got a cab, but then got stuck in traffic, finally picked up Gelman and Laurie and, by the time we got to the theater, it was a few minutes after six.

And guess what.

The movie had started on time!

And guess what else.

NO SEATS!

Then one of the movie publicists came up and said, "Oh, I saved a couple seats for you!" They were pretty good seats, too. But I told him, "I'm not going in unless Gelman gets a couple of seats as well."

So they also got a couple of seats—IN THE NEXT THEATER AROUND THE CORNER, IN THE SECOND ROW AND THEY WEREN'T TOGETHER.

I think they still have neck cramps.

> JOY: *Well, I asked Michael if he was upset with me. He said, "No, but I've learned a lesson: We'll meet you two wherever we're going, so if you show up late, it's not my problem." And it isn't his problem, Regis. It's your problem!*

You're absolutely right, and what a problem!

JOY: And you're stuck with it.

I know, I know.

MAKE ROOM (ONSTAGE) FOR DADDY

A STORY FROM J.J. PHILBIN:

The year I turned sixteen, I was in tenth grade and everyone I knew was throwing a Sweet Sixteen party. I really wanted my party to stand out, to be terrific. So my mom and I brainstormed and came up with what we thought was a great party. We rented a huge space downtown, got a band and the whole gimmick of the party was that kids could sing karaoke all night. (This was at the beginning of the whole karaoke craze.)

Now, there's always that awkward first hour when people are just milling around, looking uncomfortable. And, of course, my parents were there to check things out. Suddenly, I looked up and, to my absolute horror, saw that my dad had climbed up on the stage. I thought, "Oh, no. Oh, no. What's he doing?" And then I saw him looking at the song selection on the karaoke machine.

At first I thought, Well, maybe he's just going to sing karaoke, which would be embarrassing, but not that embarrassing. I mean, that is what we're all doing here. But he started doing these vocal exercises. The same ones we used to hear him doing in the bathroom at home—these sort of very loud and grating ohhhh meeee aaah eeeeee oooh noooooooos. And then we would all run for cover.

So he started throwing out a few eee oooh nooos up onstage and I thought, Well, that's it. It occured to me that he saw this as free rehearsal time for his nightclub act! I couldn't believe it.

And then the music started and he began to sing "My Way." I glanced around the room and these kids were just giving him the evil eye, that classic look of disdain reserved for parents making fools of themselves. I wanted to die. Then he moved on to "Calendar Girl"—he did everything in his repertoire.

I thought, This can't be happening to me! *I rushed to Mom in tears. "This is a nightmare! Can't you make him stop?" She said, "I don't think so." She was sympathetic, but basically powerless because Dad paid for the whole thing and figured why not work on a couple numbers while he was there. He said later, "I was trying to get the party moving for you!" But, at the time, the only moving I could think about was moving to a different state!*

GREASE WAS *NOT* THE WORD, ALL RIGHT!

A STORY FROM JOANNA PHILBIN:

Just like so many little girls of our generation, J.J. and I had this huge obsession with Grease. *It was sort of a seminal film for us, and we listened to the soundtrack night and day. We knew every single word to every single song. We had it on an album, we had it on tape, we had the sheet music, we had everything. And one day, we noticed that the album was mysteriously missing. Vanished. Could not be found. And it really threw us all into this huge search.*

We tore the place apart, looking through every corner to try to locate this Grease *album. We asked everyone in the house about it constantly, every day, all the time. Mom helped us look around. Dad seemed a little less interested—*

"Dad, have you seen the Grease *album?"*

"No, honey, I haven't seen it. I have no idea. No."

Finally, we just sort of gave up.

But then J.J. and I happened to be talking about this just the other day—

only twenty years later! Because we always had our suspicions. So we asked him point-blank, since the statute of limitations by now was up.

He finally confessed: He threw it away.

"I'm sorry, honey, BUT I JUST COULDN'T TAKE IT ANYMORE! ALL DAY, ALL NIGHT, OVER AND OVER AND OVER AGAIN—ENOUGH!"

Anyway, we're getting him the CD for his birthday.

A TALE OF TWO CHRISTMASES—
(OR: I'M SO GLAD WE HAD THIS TIME TOGETHER!)

We all have favorite Christmas stories, but let me tell you about two memorable Christmases that took place, back to back, in Los Angeles. This was during the mid-seventies. Joy and I had purchased a home in the Hancock Park area formerly owned by comedian Harvey Korman, who had been a great longtime stalwart on *The Carol Burnett Show.* Of course, in Los Angeles, you're nobody unless you live in the former home of a famous person. So, one Christmas Day, at about three o'clock in the afternoon, we sat down to our holiday dinner. Joy's mother was there. My mother was there. So were the kids, of course.

Suddenly, the doorbell rang.

We weren't expecting anybody else.

But I opened the door and there was Harvey Korman with his son and daughter. Harvey said, "Do you mind if we come in and just look around?" He had been back in the neighborhood, having dinner with cousins, and he must have felt a flood of wistful memories. What else could I do but invite him in? I figured it would take a quick five minutes to walk him through his old house. A little holiday nostalgia. I understood completely.

But Harvey lingered in each room, becoming more and more nostalgic. And bittersweet. His eyes grew misty. Upstairs, his kids explored their old bedrooms. In the master bedroom, I saw a couple of tears well up in Harvey's eyes. Then his kids turned to him and said, "Why did we ever move? Why did you take us away from here? We loved this house! It was our house." Suddenly, they were engaged in kind of a heart-wrenching family caucus. I felt for them. I really did. But it was Christmas and my mood was now plummeting by the minute.

Finally, the Kormans left and the Philbins ate a somber meal.

One Christmas later, it happened all over again. Just as we were sitting down to dinner, the doorbell rang. I looked at Joy and said, "Naw, it couldn't be." But it was. There on the doorstep were Harvey and his two kids. "Gee," he said, tentatively, "can we come in and look around?"

Of course, Harvey, please. Anything you want.

I welcomed them in and let them wander through the house. Again, he shared memories with us, recounting golden days of his years on the premises. And again, his kids got upset. "Why did we move?" they asked him. "You changed our lives!" It was like watching a *Sally Jessy Raphael* show explode before your eyes. Finally, they left.

And, once again, our family fell into a gloomy funk.

Nobody felt like talking.

We ate in grim silence.

The next Christmas, we went out to dinner.

I Have to Get Up Five Times a Night—
WHAT DO YOU CARE?

You want the truth? You may know it already—since it seems that *everyone* knows already! But, okay, here it is: I don't sleep straight through the night anymore. I haven't had a good night's sleep since I was about thirteen! **The problem is the prostate.** I long ago made the mistake of talking about it on the air with Kathie Lee. What *glee* she took in regularly demanding the overnight total of how many times I'd used the bathroom—while trying to rest myself for another morning of battle with Itself! The woman was obsessed! Eventually, I had to stop addressing the subject. It got to the point where *everyone* was taking count. How dare they invade my privacy? I'm a private guy! But the point remains: I just can't get a good night's sleep.

SO I FOUND MYSELF
A SENSITIVE UROLOGIST

Well, you've gotta do something! I went to see a urologist who came highly recommended for his *sensitivity*. And that's what I want in my urologist. Experience—I don't care about it! But *sensitivity*— that's my guy! And this guy was a saint and a respected teacher to boot. Anyway, it was just supposed to be a "get acquainted" visit. (Gelman, meanwhile, had wanted to strap tiny cameras on both me and the doc to catch all the action. No way! Gelman doesn't understand *sensitivity!*)

But, as I was going over to the doctor's office, I felt terrific. I said to myself, "Why am I going? I feel great!" Okay, I was going because of a symptom: I was getting up four or five times during the night. *So I had four or five symptoms!* Fine! You reach a point in your life where you're continually getting up during the night and suddenly you're always exhausted in the morning.

So—despite these *symptoms*—I was saying to myself, "This is ridiculous!" I pushed open the door to this medical building and went inside and saw people in there who really needed medical attention. And, again, you say to yourself, "Forget it! I'm healthy, I'm fine, everything's great." But I had told the doctor that I was coming, so there was no turning back. All I wanted to do was sit down and talk to him and let him talk to me. We were gonna get acquainted. **It's a first date, *all right*?**

But before you see a doctor anymore, they have to extract blood. It's like you shake hands with the nurse and suddenly she's taking blood out of your arm. Right off the bat! Blood! I don't like blood at all. But she was pretty good, this nurse. Then they needed another sample. Do I have to spell it out for you? You know what I'm referring to. It involves a cup. A very little cup!

This cup was so small that I got nervous that I might have an overflow!

Anyway, the cup is filled, the blood is taken, so finally I meet my Sensitive Urologist and we talked. I told him what the problem was and he was very nice, very . . . sensitive. And he said, "Let's go in the other room." I said, "*Why*, why are we going in the other room?" He said, "Well, I have to give you an examination."

"Why?! I told you what the problem is! Now you tell me what you can do for me!"

"No," he said, "we must go into the other room."

So we went into the other room. And we talked, gently, quietly—and, yes, *sensitively.*

"How did you get started in television?" he asked.

"Well, I was an NBC page, I was a stagehand, then a stage manager . . ." And on and on . . . *and on.* Suddenly, he had turned into Charlie Rose doing a career retrospective!

Then, out of the corner of my eye, I saw him going for the bag of gloves. I said, "What are you doing? What's over there?!!" He smiled and said nothing. **He was putting on his glove!** Now, I have resisted this examination all of my life, so I said, "Look, I hardly know you. Are you sure? How long are you gonna be in there?"

"Two seconds," he assured me.

I said, "I'm gonna count. One, two and that's it! You're out!"

And that's all it was. But from those two seconds, he could tell everything about me! My middle name!! MY MOTHER'S MAIDEN NAME!! HOW WOULD HE KNOW THAT!!? HOW COULD HE KNOW THAT!!!??? FROM TWO SECONDS!!!! Talk about your sensitivity!

Anyway, I was very brave. I sucked it up, so to speak. And he did what had to be done. Then he left and I felt totally humiliated. No—I felt totally **VIOLATED!** But I also did what I had to do and I went back into the other office where he told me, "You're fine. Everything's fine."

Which I was trying to tell him all along!

But there was another punchline to this whole trauma. Instead of suggesting surgery or something else to correct my *symptoms*, he said that I just needed a little prescription that would stop the night problem so I could finally sleep. So I filled his prescription and that night I took this pill before bed.

Then I got in bed and waited for something to happen. Here's what happened: I got the *worst night's sleep of my life!*

And, honest to God, I still got up five times!!

So much for sensitivity.

JUST GIVE IT TO ME WITH A SMILE, DOC!

I hate going to see my doctor. I have no problem with him personally—his name is Jeffrey Borer and he's a great doctor and a lovely man. But he's got those numbers in his hand and I know he's going to say, "Hey, Mr. Bigshot, your cholesterol is too high. What're we gonna do?" Like I said, wonderful guy, great doctor. The only thing is, when he's looking over all the charts and test results—just before he tells me the verdict—my heart starts *pounding*.

I tell you, I CAN'T TAKE IT!

Just give it to me and give it to me with a SMILE!

And, anyway, no matter what he tells me, it's all genetic.

I'm fighting a genetic battle and losing.

I've been exercising and cutting down on fatty foods. But you can't fight nature—and nature wants me to have high cholesterol. And even when my cholesterol is down, my blood pressure is up. And *why?* Just why do you think my blood pressure is up? Could it be that spending an hour every day for fifteen years sitting next to you-know-who might have something to do with it? It slowly wears a man down . . .

I COULD EXPLODE AT ANY MINUTE.

Because of this, I endure a day each year that most men wouldn't be brave enough to tell you about. In fact, I rarely say a word about it. I keep it to myself. I'm talking about my annual physical. Stress test, blood test—the works. For my last one, they shot me with something in each arm that adheres to the red blood cells because that's what they were tracking. (*Needles* again! I hate those needles!) The next day, I got the results of my blood test. And I have to tell you, **I was a little concerned about my testosterone level.** So was Joy. All you hear about lately is how important testosterone is.

Well, I was expecting either a BIG testosterone number . . . or none at all. I didn't find out what the actual number was, but they told me it was "normal." A very boring "normal."

JOY: Well, I learned what your number was. I talked to Dr. Borer about it because I just wanted to know what's in store for me. He said that your level right now is 57—the normal range being between 50-210. The way I look at it, you're just barely squeaking by. Honestly.

How could that be? I'm 57 out of 210? Don't they know about my chain saw?

JOY: Well, there are additional tests you could take to measure it. There's a gonadal test you might enjoy.

Gonadal?
And you thought the Sopranos talked rough!
Come to think of it, maybe Joy is borrowing my testosterone.

WHY MY BLOOD PRESSURE TRULY SOARS

All right, I've blamed everyone for it at one time or another. And I've probably blamed the beloved former morning cohost more than anyone else. But I was just kidding about that (for the most part). Here, though, is the real reason my blood pressure count is often too high:

The renovations at New York Hospital.

There has been so much renovating going on at this hospital that I CAN'T FIND MY DOCTOR'S OFFICE ANYMORE.

In fact, I'd like to give the New York Hospital chiefs a small recommendation to factor into their ongoing renovation plans—

TEAR IT DOWN!!!

I'll say it again:

TEAR IT DOWN AND BUILD IT OVER AGAIN!

I get angry just thinking about trying to find my doctor's office over there. Everything's in chaos. I've wandered down each and every hallway of those buildings—hours of searching, climbing, asking directions, retracing my footsteps, over and over and over again. Certain corridors are blocked off. There are dozens of different elevator banks. From one visit to the next, you cannot take the same route to get to where you need to go. I break out in cold sweats. I pant hard. I lose stamina. Because the hospital changes every day!

I've tried a new plan of attack. I know his office is on the fourth floor—*that's all I know!* So I get up to the fourth floor somehow. I know he's on the fourth floor. I don't know *where* on the fourth floor, but he's there somewhere.

So I go to the nearest phone and I say to the receptionist lady, "Where am I right now?"

"You're on 4-21-14A."

Fine, good. I pick up the phone. I call Dr. Borer's office. I say "Look, I'm here, I'm in 4-21-14A. *Please come and get me!*"

They send a bloodhound and a guide holding a little sign that says, "Follow me, Regis."

But it doesn't matter.

Because by the time I get to him, my blood pressure is out of control! And that's when he always says to me, "I don't know what's wrong with you."

Here's a hint, Doc:

TEAR IT DOWN!

OH, AND BY THE WAY . . .

Here's another hint to anybody who takes my blood pressure:

When you wrap that thing around my arm—that thing I hate that *grips* and *grips* you—and while you're looking at the reading, please don't say the following things:

"*Huhhhhhh!*"

"*Uh-ohhhh . . .*"

And "*Wow!*"

IT'S NOT TOO MUCH TO ASK, IS IT?

NO COLONOSCOPY FOR ME!

I don't care what part of the body we're talking about. I don't want doctors doing *anything* inside of me if I can help it. The actual technical term for any such medical procedure is "invasive."

YOU'D BETTER BELIEVE IT'S *INVASIVE!*

I don't like *invasive*.

Do something on the outside of me—I won't complain.

But invasive—no way!

And, for the record, I've never been able to imagine anything that could be quite as invasive as the dreaded *colonoscopy!* C-O-L-O-N-O-S-C-O-P-Y—it's a *terrible* word. I cringe every time I hear it. Unfortunately, Kathie Lee loved to say it to me every chance she got. Nothing pleased the woman more than the idea of me getting a colonoscopy! (I'm sure she meant well—but then again, we're talking about a COLONOSCOPY here! Show me a little mercy.)

I've never had one and I never want one. Oh, sure, I've had something called a sigmoidoscopy—where they took a little peek up in there. But never the WHOLE PEEK, if you know what I mean.

Even Gelman told me that he once had a colonoscopy. "They put you out," he said. "It's very easy." Sure. For him, it was easy. You couldn't put me out far enough.

Even the great Notre Dame basketball coach Digger Phelps once came on the show not long after he had a colonoscopy. I wanted his version of the horror story, which was all I needed to know.

ME: Come on, Digger, you can tell me. You had it done?

D.P.: Absolutely!

ME: What was it like?

D.P.: It's kind of like doing the Hindu rope trick blindfolded.

ME: The HINDU ROPE TRICK!?!

D.P.: And they kept pumping air through it—"More air, more air."

ME: They pump air through the Hindu rope! I don't want to hear any more. Never mention this to me again!! Anyone!

THE SENATOR WHO SENT ME FOR AN ENEMA!

You want embarrassing? Let me take you back about five years to an episode that ranks about as high on the embarrassment scale as anything I've ever experienced. It was the kind of thing that only happens when I'm left to my own devices. Joy had flown off one Sunday afternoon to travel around Spain with J.J. So it was just me all alone in our old apartment on Park Avenue. I don't know exactly what I'd eaten after she left, but I woke up at four in the morning that Monday feeling a case of the grippers clenching at my stomach.

Oh, the dreaded grippers!

Those searing abdominal cramps from hell.

What a way to start the week.

But I went to work and got through our *Live!* show, trying to disguise the fact that I was in total agony. Before the show, I'd taken a big dose of Imodium AD in the prop room. Then I took a second swig right after the show. Gelman warned me that it's pretty potent stuff, but I did it anyway. Didn't help. The grippers just continued gripping me throughout the day.

Meanwhile, Claudia Cohen's office called to say that she wanted me to join her that night for a party honoring the architect Charles Gwathmey. (Claudia, of course, covers parties and celebrity events for our show and does it like no one else.) I agreed, figuring I'd feel better by then. By late afternoon, though, my grippers had gotten so intense that I just wanted to call and cancel. But I also didn't want to leave her unescorted. Anyway, she called me around eight just as she was leaving her apartment. And that's when she mentioned that she was also bringing a date—New York Senator Alfonse D'Amato. (The two of them had just recently started seeing each other.) Naturally, if I had known she had an escort, I would have canceled!

But she was on her way and there was no way out!

Anyway, they picked me up and we headed over to the party at the Racquet Club on Park Avenue. Senator Al seemed to be in good spirits—especially now that he and Claudia had been hitting it off. They were giggling and laughing—and, meanwhile, MY GRIPPERS WERE GETTING STRONGER BY THE MINUTE.

We got to the party, where the paparazzi made a rush for the senator and Claudia. Since they were the latest "item" in town, the flashbulbs didn't stop popping. Everywhere we moved at the party, cameras kept going off—and shooting pains through my stomach. *But I kept smiling—*like a good third wheel is supposed to. Then they wanted to leave the event and head over to Elaine's for a little dinner.

Meanwhile, I'm now feeling terrible and also angry with myself for ever going out in the first place. I JUST WANT TO GO HOME. That feeling is never stronger than when we zoom right past my apartment house.

But I'm trapped!

At Elaine's, we sit at the same table where Joy and I shot our famous scene with Bobby De Niro in *Night and the City*. (All right, it was only three minutes long, but it deserves to be famous!) Even that memory doesn't help. Claudia orders fried calamari and fried zucchini—*which also doesn't help*—while I sip a Perrier.

Finally she takes mercy, realizes I'm sick and starts suggesting remedies for my problem. Claudia is very health-conscious and doctor-oriented. She has just the doctor for your every ache and pain. Anyway, my troubles now have more to do with those swigs of Imodium AD this morning than anything else.

Gelman was right about that stuff.

The truth is that I am *blocked*.

Or constipated, as they say.

Claudia instantly prescribes an enema.

I'm in terror. An enema!

I hadn't had an enema in half a century!

Senator Al nods and says, "A Fleet enema. Absolutely no problem." Suddenly, one of the most powerful senators in the country is weighing in on the enema vote! But he's deeply concerned and calls over one of his security men who's lingering at the bar. He tells him, "I want you to take Regis home and stop at the drugstore on the way and buy him an enema."

The security guy's eyes widen and he bellows:

"AN ENEMA?!"

Why is it that at moments like these all sound stops in a room? Everything just gets quiet while that word echoes.

And echoes.

I shrink in my seat.

A nearby table of ten turns to look at me. I wave a little. But there's no sense arguing with the senator. I decide to just get out of there and take my chances on the way home.

In the car, I tell the guy that I really don't need an enema. "Oh, no," he says, overruling me. He's a retired homicide detective who has his orders from Senator Al.

"He said an enema, we get you an enema!"

We pull up to a Love pharmacy on Eighty-sixth Street and go inside. (Yes—to add to the humiliation—I am being shadowed by my security detail, who won't leave me alone until he sees me buy my enema!) It's around ten o'clock, but the store is more crowded than I'd hoped. And, of course, the customers are surprised to see me—and even more surprised to see me take a Fleet enema off the shelf.

Why didn't I just stay home?

AND WHY AM I STANDING IN LINE WAITING TO PAY FOR AN ENEMA?

I get it paid for, but not before the cashier takes a good long look at me. Back to the car, on to home, where I get out and try to hide the purchase from the doorman. I can't wait to get inside my own apartment. All of this aggravation has intensified my grippers.

I need relief!

I study the green-and-white Fleet box, with a diagram of two suitable positions in which to administer the product. Well, what do I have to lose?

I assume position B and, let's just say, I try and I fail.

That's right, I failed at my own enema.

Go ahead, mock me—I don't care.

Just like life, enemas ain't that easy.

LOCK YOUR UNISEX BATHROOM DOOR, ALL RIGHT?

So I had this cough and it was a miserable cough, it was a wretched cough. For weeks, I coughed and coughed, driving everybody crazy (especially a certain redhead fated to live with me). Day and night, I coughed my brains out, then coughed some more. But you can't surrender, you can't stop living life. You've just got to get it off your chest, otherwise you can't talk or, when you do talk, you sound like Vito Corleone.

Anyway, it reached its peak one night on vacation out in Beverly Hills when Joy and I went to dinner with our good friends Peter and Alice Lassally at a dynamite restaurant called Drai's Cafe. Very elegant, very modern and well lit and brimming with showbiz power players. So we sit down and, of course, I go straight into a coughing fit. Now, you know how annoying it is to be sitting in a restaurant, surrounded by people, when the phlegm starts rising and you can't stop it.

So I did the gentlemanly thing—I excused myself and went to find the rest rooms, where I could hack away in privacy with a little dignity intact, thank you very much. The main rest rooms were on the bottom floor, but I spotted a small sign on the wall that said "Additional rest rooms upstairs." Perfect. I don't want to bother anybody in the main men's room with my infernal coughing. I go upstairs and see just one door with two little symbols affixed to it—one of a man . . . and the other of a *madame!* Uh-oh. Might be trouble. **It's one of those unisex bathrooms.** Welcome to the future! But I figure that I'm safely upstairs where nobody else would bother to go.

Anyway, I give the door a little knock, because you don't just walk in there not knowing what you'll find! What am I gonna do—jiggle the lock first and barge in? **NO, I'M POLITE! I KNOCK!** Nobody responded. I go inside. And I lock the door. This lock was a little weird, though—modern, technological, complex!—and I had trouble. I mean, I thought it was secured; I tried the door, it seemed okay. And then I proceeded to cough my brains out. A major fit—*unpleasant!*—but I cleansed my chest. Then before leaving, I decide that rather than having to get up again from the table, I might as well use the room for what it was meant to be used for. **After all, the door is locked!**

But I still go to that door again because I'm not completely sure about this lock-of-tomorrow. I twist and retwist it—still locked. Fine. And while I'm standing against the wall doing my business, I hear footsteps coming up to the door. *Loud footsteps!* I'm saying to myself, "Thank God that door is locked!" Then I hear . . . **A HAND ON THE DOOR!!!** And the handle is turning . . .

I'm thinking, *NOO! NO!* I can't believe it! And then I hear the door *opening!* That stupid lock never held! Now I'm facing the wall and I'm trying to peek over my shoulder—is it a man or is it a woman?

Honest to God, a *woman* walks right in!

I said, "DON'T YOU KNOCK?!" And instantly she turned and walked out. Now, if that were me walking in on a woman, I'd *vanish!* I'd be down those stairs and back at my table like I'd never left! Or maybe I'd just run from the restaurant. Do you think I'd stand out there and wait for her to come out? No! I'd be *gone.*

But not her. No, not this woman. She stood outside that faulty door and waited proudly, ready to give me a look that said, "What took you so long?" But she didn't actually say that. Instead, when I came out and stared in her eyes, she said: *"Regis Philbin!!"* I died. And then she said, **"I DIDN'T SEE A THING."** Oh, really? Is that supposed to make me feel better?

Yes, it was me, lady! I'm sorry you had to see me standing there at the john—but that's my life!

The moral: You must knock on those unisex doors! And then make sure that the stupid lock works! When you have your faith in a lock, you should be able to hear the Russian Army coming up those stairs and rest assured that they're not going to get in that room because . . . the LOCK is LOCKED!

Letterman Gave Me the FINGER!

TOP TEN SIGNS REGIS PHILBIN IS NUTS

10. He's actually gone on one of those lame Carnival cruises.

9. Keeps showing up for work in full *Cats* makeup.

8. One minute you're having a civilized conversation and the next minute the old coot's on the floor doing push-ups.

7. Richard Simmons found smothered under a two-ton pile of Regis's workout videos.

6. Now kicks off each morning show by biting head off chicken.

5. Claims the CIA has been sending satellite beams into his pants.

4. Last week spotted naked in Central Park with bottle of scotch screaming, "Where's Gelman?"

3. Never changed his weird-ass name.

2. Every couple of years, just for fun, he switches Kathie Lee's birth control pills with Tic Tacs.

1. Come on, look at the guy.

Sure, we kid around with each other a lot, but whenever David Letterman needs me, I'm there. I rush over to that Ed Sullivan Theater on Broadway and do whatever his *Late Show* producers tell me to do. I can't begin to count the number of times they've made me run up and down the aisles like a madman in order to wake up their audience and rescue a dying bit.

BECAUSE IF I COUNTED, I'D GET VERY DEPRESSED!

But I know David can't always entertain late-night America all by himself. He's a tremendously talented broadcaster, but—just like me— he's only one man. So I do whatever I can to help out. That's why his executive producer Rob Burnett gave me a special title that holds true to this day . . .

THEY CALL ME "THE SHOW SAVER."

That's right—the Show Saver!

Having said all that, you'd think that David and I would have some kind of a deep, meaningful bond by now. All I've ever wanted to do was be this guy's friend. He needs a friend! We all need friends! But he's a very private person and it's hard to penetrate that tough exterior of his. Chuck Grodin and I have tried to get him to come out to dinner in Connecticut with us and maybe get together with the great Jack Paar. Every time we bring it up, however, HE LAUGHS IN OUR FACES. Oh, we get along fine, especially after I guided him through his big heart-bypass scare. But there was one night when I feared it was all over between me and the big man.

Let me tell you what happened:

They sent for the Show Saver again, so there I was back at the theater. Right away, they rushed me as usual into this little backstage cubicle—their Green Room—which is always crowded with people. In fact, there are usually more people standing around in that room than all the people we have on our *Live!* staff put together. And they all just stare at each other, doing nothing. I hate that room.

Anyway, since I know the routine so well, I figure that they want me to go to Makeup, which is on the fifth floor. So I walk down the hallway to take the elevator up there. I get in the elevator and the door is just about to shut when one of David's minions runs up and says, "No, they want you back in the Green Room." Okay, fine. Out of the elevator, back to the Green Room. I'm just about to sit down when the same kid informs me, "They want you up in Makeup."

WHICH ONE IS IT?

So I head back down the hall to the elevator and, on the way, people are yelling, "Hey, Regis, how you doing?" Show Saver always gets the Letterman troops worked up. They know it's going to be an exciting night if Show Saver is in the building.

Up on the fifth floor, more people are yelling my name from all sides as I walk toward Makeup. I smile and wave and keep moving. The makeup lady fixes me up, then she leaves to do David's makeup while the hair guy works me over. But when the makeup gal returns from doing Letterman, she tells me, "He's very *upset* with you."

"With *me*? Why? What happened?"

"He says you snubbed him."

"I *snubbed* him? When?"

"Out in the corridor, he said hello to you and you didn't respond to him."

I say, "Honest to God, I didn't see him! Maybe my head was down because they were shuttling me back and forth. I missed him. But do me a favor—when you see him tomorrow, tell him I didn't snub him. I DIDN'T EVEN SEE HIM!"

Anyway, it's time to tape the show. Dr. Joyce Brothers and I are supposed to come out onstage to present a mock Academy Award for the best-looking guy at the pizzeria around the corner. One of the five contestants happens to be Dame Judi Dench—and she loses. Letterman selects the winner and that's my cue to emerge from the wings with Dr.

Joyce to give out the award. But as I step out from behind the curtains with those lights beaming down on us, I spot Letterman sitting behind his desk, in semi-shadow.

But I can clearly see that he's making an obscene gesture.

AT ME!!!

It involved the use of his middle finger!

Yes, Letterman was flipping Show Saver the bird!!!

Gelman did that to me once, but he was hung over. Other than that, no one has ever dared! At least, not on national television. I mean, New York is the capital of obscene gestures. But on network TV? Still, it was very funny.

Then I realized, *Maybe he's not kidding. Maybe he means it. Maybe he really believes that I snubbed him!*

So we begin this award bit and, as we're waiting for the winner to run over from the pizza joint and collect his trophy, David walks up to me and says, "YOU SNUBBED ME!"

I mean, he was *serious* about this!

We hand over the award to the pizza guy, then Paul Shaffer and the CBS Orchestra started playing so loudly that I couldn't have a conversation with Dave. I couldn't even defend myself.

But, in the days that followed, this alleged snubbing incident weighed on me. *How could I snub him if I didn't see him?* I swear, he's like the Phantom of the Opera around that place! No one ever sees him until he walks onstage. I've *never* seen him backstage! Ever. I told Chuck Grodin about all this and, a couple weeks later, he went on *The Late Show* and thought it would be a scream to discuss it with Letterman on the air.

Chuck tried to explain that I didn't snub Dave because I DIDN'T SEE HIM. And that was when Letterman—on national television—called me "a pantywaist liar."

A PANTYWAIST LIAR?!

What does that even mean?

And Grodin sat there and agreed with him!

He said, "Uh-huh, you're right about that."

Hey, thanks for ever bringing it up, Chuck.

Meanwhile, I'm at home watching this in bed, not bothering anyone, not even Joy.

Still, it got under my skin, it festered inside, so I talked about it on *Live!* the next morning:

ME: A *pantywaist* liar? He thinks I'm a sissy!

K.L.: This is pathetic. You boys should grow up.

ME: It *is* pathetic! What should I call him? COME ON, GELMAN, COME UP WITH SOMETHING FOR ME TO CALL HIM!

G: You should challenge him to a fight. Remember when Geraldo boxed somebody?

ME: No, he's too big. He's got too much reach. But I tell you what—why doesn't my producer fight his producer? There you go!

K.L.: That's right. Why should you put your own life in peril? Put Gelman's life in peril!

ME: And I can play the Burgess Meredith role in *Rocky* one more time! I'll be the corner man! "Get up, Gelman, get back in there!"

K.L.: I'm glad you guys aren't role models for my children. So pathetic!

Gelman, of course, backed out of that one. But, months later, I figured that our feud was over, so I went back on the Letterman show to talk about *Millionaire* and have some laughs. Everything went fine until the end of my segment. This time, he casually threw another insult at me. This time, he called me a *fruit*.

A FRUIT!

Here I had turned the other cheek because I still wanted to be his friend and now I'm a fruit!

Again, I forgave him, but the funny part was that my old Bronx pal Freakin' Finelli saw that show and got upset. Freakin' takes name-calling very seriously. Freakin' doesn't like the sound of *fruit*, okay? He called me up and said, "Reege, the guys in the neighborhood don't like it. The guys in the neighborhood wanna know where David lives."

I said, "Easy, Freakin'. He was only kidding!"

Freakin' wasn't so sure.

But, from the start, Dave was one of the biggest supporters of *Millionaire* and his writers have cooked up all kinds of bits based on the show, including this Top Ten List from the week of our debut:

From the Home Office in Wahoo, Nebraska, It's the Top Ten List:

TOP TEN COMMON RESPONSES TO THE QUESTION "WHO WANTS TO BE A MILLIONAIRE?"

10. "I do."
9. "You bet your sweet ass I do."
8. "Sweet screamin' monkeys, that's a stupid question."
7. "No thanks, I think I'll just keep working here at Radio Shack."
6. "What part of Regis Philbin would I have to touch?"
5. "Not me. I'm Bill Gates and that would be a colossal step backwards."

4. "Who do I have to kill?"
3. "Only if I can get it all in nickels."
2. "Since I'm the Dalai Lama, I am not interested in worldly riches. . . . Ah, screw it, where's the cash?"
1. "How many crappy magazines do I have to subscribe to?"

And then came that mid-January night when I was sitting there next to his desk and he confessed to me—and to all of America—that he was worried about going in the next morning for an angiogram and possible heart procedure. He called me his "role model" and asked me all about the angioplasty I had years earlier . . .

D.L.: Were you scared?

ME: I was scared, yeah.

D.L.: Because they take that thing and go right up inside your—

ME: They run it right up your groin muscle.

D.L.: Right. Very close to your deal!

ME: Well, in my case, it was too close to my deal. In fact, that was a big deal! It's not so funny when it's you!

D.L.: No, it's not funny. I don't know why you're laughing and kidding around here!

Well, the big man was understandably rattled about the whole thing and, as it turned out, the next day he received a very successful quintuple bypass at New York Hospital. While he recovered, I was honored to step in and host some of his retrospective *Late Show Backstage* replacement programs. And then five short weeks after his surgery, there he was back on the air and, once again, I was sitting right there next to him, picking up where we left off—and trying to pry loose some of the details of what he had gone through . . .

> ME: Now let me ask you something—when they had you on the gurney
> and they were wheeling you down the hallway, what were your final
> thoughts before you went under? Did you think of me at all? Anything?
>
> D.L.: Actually, I was thinking about Joy . . .

But there's one more twist to this story that I haven't shared before.

Oddly enough, about two months after David's big comeback show, I very quietly had another angioplasty. Not a big deal. Just one night in New York Hospital, in and out. While I was there, the doctor who had operated on Letterman came by and offhandedly mentioned, "You know, you're in the same room and the same bed that Dave had."

I said, "Really? That's funny! Let's call and tell him!"

It was eight o'clock at night, so I figured he was probably lurking around his office. I dialed the number and an unfamiliar female voice answered—probably an intern.

"Hi," I said, "this is Regis Philbin and I'd like to talk to David Letterman."

She said, "Yeah—*and I'm Kathie Lee!*"

"Look, it really is Regis Philbin."

"*Oh, come on!*"

Of course, she's probably been trained to ward off every moron in America who tries to call the big boy.

So I tried a different tack:

"Is Diamond there?" (I hoped the mention of his executive assistant, Laurie Diamond, would work as some sort of secret password. Diamond—as everyone calls her—has always been my link to him.)

"No, she's not."

Now, here I was, recovering from an angioplasty in the same bed that he had and trying on a whim to have some fun with him—AND I WAS GETTING NOWHERE! But I hung in there. Then, another girl came on the line and I tried all over again—

"Yeah, *this is really Regis!* I'm here in New York Hospital. AND I WANT TO TALK TO DAVID! Please! *Show me a little mercy here!*"

Finally, he got on the phone—

AND *HE* DOESN'T BELIEVE IT'S ME, EITHER!

I said, "Look, this is so anticlimactic now! I'm in the same bed you were in and your cracker crumbs are still here! What do you care?" And only then, very cautiously, did he loosen up and play along.

But he must have felt bad about the whole thing. Because the next day, one of his girls phoned my office and said to my assistant Pam, "If Regis wants to call again tonight, it's fine."

I told Pam, "No, Regis has called already. He ain't calling again, thank you."

At least he didn't call me a pantywaist.

He/She Said, SHE/HE SAID

Τ he first time it happened was Halloween 1994. For our special
Halloween broadcast that morning, Gelman had decided that I would
dress up and become Kathie Lee, and she would dress up and become
me. We would spend the entire hour on the air completely in character
and do our best to drive each other crazy. (Frankly, we had been doing
that for nine years already *without* wearing costumes—but when Gelman
gets a new idea, there's no talking him out of it.) So, quite literally, Kathie
Lee and I stepped into each other's shoes. And I'll tell you, I definitely
got the short end of the stick on that one! High heels are *painful!*

I remember coming in a little early that morning to be outfitted in my
Kathie Lee drag ensemble. Actually, what I remember most about that
was how my padded bra intrigued everyone in the makeup room. Arlette,
the makeup lady, was the first one to take a feel. I couldn't believe it!
Then two other female staff members gave me a fondling. How dare they?
Finally, Gelman came in and helped himself, too. I was shocked. They
made me feel so cheap, so easy, so tawdry. Like a piece of meat! I wanted to slap them all. But, then again, it *was* kind of exciting.

I'll tell you, though, three hundred sixty-four days of the year, Kathie
Lee is quite the looker, every inch a woman. But between you and me,

she was the STRANGEST LOOKING MAN I'D EVER SEEN! She came out wearing a brown wig and one of my jackets and a tie—and somehow bore an odd resemblance, I thought, to my cousin Chris Boscia. It was a little terrifying! On the other hand, I made quite a handsome woman. At least from the thighs down—what with my hairless legs and perfect size-eight feet. Otherwise—in wig, makeup, pearls, earrings, pantyhose, blouse and skirt—I looked more like Julia Child than Kathie Lee. The only thing I couldn't really get used to was the draft up my skirt. You never realize how cold it really is until you get a shot of frigid air up there.

But we did get a lot of reaction. From the minute I sat down on her stool, I felt like a channeler, spewing all the things I had been hearing come out of her mouth every morning for years. I must admit, it was quite cathartic! I opened my locket to show a picture of my husband, Frank, the Love Machine. I talked about bathing with Cody and Cassidy. I talked about giving money to charities and sang lyrics from those Carnival Cruises commercials—*"IF YOU COULD SEE ME NOW . . ."* I covered every base.

And she kept right up with me—delivering every word in a slightly annoyed tone, complaining, sounding excitable and overwhelmed and put-upon . . .

FRANKLY, SHE NEVER SOUNDED BETTER IN HER LIFE!

What I enjoyed most was sitting back and watching her handle my regular duties—keeping the conversation moving when it slowed, getting to the trivia question, introducing the guests, giving Gelman the occasional shot, holding up the headlines, keeping me in check while still giving me a chance to occasionally blurt, *"I love you, Cody!"* But, surreal as it was, the show instantly became one of the most talked-about hours we'd ever done.

Which made it all the more amazing that Gelman waited *five more years* before we did it all over again, on Halloween 1999. But there was a lot of new material for us to get out of our systems and have fun with.

Kathie Lee came out in a dark *Millionaire* suit combination and I was fighting for my life all over again in those heels and panty hose. And, true to character, I made my entrance singing my head off . . .

> **ME [AS HER]: WAAAAHHHHHHHHHHHHHHHHHH!**
>
> **K.L.: [AS ME]: SHE'S OUTTA CONTROL!**
>
> **ME: Oh, *Reeeeeeeeggge!***
>
> **K.L.: All right, all right, get over there and sit down! You know your place!**
>
> **ME: Wait a minute, Reege, let me get this hair out of my face! Okay!**
>
> **K.L.: You know what this weekend is, don't ya?**
>
> **ME: What?**
>
> **K.L.: It's the Notre Dame–Navy game! You know what Notre Dame's gonna do to Navy!? You know what you can do with this, don't ya? Here's your Navy!**
>
> **ME: Well, we had a dinner party last night.**
>
> **K.L.: Who cares? Who cares?**
>
> **ME: President Ford and Mrs. Ford were there. So was Kevin Costner. And you know who else came? John Gotti! Everybody was there except you, *Reeeeeeeeggge!***
>
> **K.L.: You know, you're an *ugly* woman! Finally, though, I gotta tell ya, somebody was smart enough to put me on their magazine cover!**

Entertainment Weekly. Yeah, after saving the network, it's the least they can do. Finally. Finally.

ME: Oh, Reege, what a good picture!

K.L.: Yeah, now I guess I gotta save *Entertainment Weekly,* too, huh?

ME: I gave Cody a bath last night!

K.L.: Who cares?!

ME: Oh, *Reeeggge* . . .where's my Frappuccino? Bobby? Bobby, my Frappuccino! [Bobby Orsillo, our prop master, brings it out] Oh, he's so handsome, isn't he, Reege?

K.L.: He's all right.

ME: Oh, you're such a man! Oh, thank you, Bobby. *Ohhh.*

K.L.: So you know, it's Halloween. . . . By the way, where's Gelman? I was out with Gelman last night.

ME: No, we don't want Gelman because Stephen Sondheim needs me on Broadway. Sondheim NEEDS me!

K.L.: Where's Gelman? Gelman! Are you ready for some Halloween things? Because it's Halloween and Gelman always wants me to show you the latest stuff. I got some stuff for you, all right? We've got this Frankenstein monster toy thing that comes alive and . . . [wrestling with toy to get it started]—GELMAN HOW DOES THIS THING WORK?!

G.: Turn it on!

K.L.: I'm tryin'! Gelman, what do I do here!? [gives up and throws it onto the floor] All right, you know, I like to scare the kids when they come to my house . . .

ME: Do you, Reeeeeeeggge? What do you do to them, Reege?

K.L.: [Now fumbling with wrapping around a jack-o'-lantern candy container that has a battery-operated ghoul hand that grabs you when you reach in for treats] HOW DO YOU GET THESE THINGS OPEN!? Gelman, open that! [He does, as usual] Now, put your hand in there, Kathie Lee!

ME: [Hand grabs her—I mean, grabs me] Oooh, scary.

K.L.: You like that? You haven't had a good feel in a long time!

ME: I have pictures of Cody and Cassidy!

K.L.: Who cares?

ME: We just took them yesterday. Here, I want to show them to you. Here are my two *little bitty* DARLINGS. Look, Reege, look!

K.L.: [Barely glancing at photos] They're all right.

ME: Look at them, they're sitting down now. And look, they're reading their favorite book, *I'm Only One Man!* Awww . . . Here's little Cody playing with his Pac-Man. And here's Cassidy picking her nose. And Cody giving Cass a little hairdo. And finally here they are fighting—Cody's beating up on Cassidy. And here's a picture of MY NEW ALBUM! Don't I look adorable on the cover?

K.L.: You got your Frappuccino, you got your kids, you got everything. But best of all, you got ME—the guy that's saving the network!

ME: OH YEAH, BABY! YEAH! Oh, Reege, I'm getting premenopausal! Reege, Reege, Reege. Last night the kids got in bed with me—oh, they're so adorable. *I love them, I love them, I love them.*

K.L.: What'd Frank have to say about that?

ME: He was snoring, he doesn't know. He was dreaming of the old days with Y. A. Tittle.

K.L.: You know, your bra is slipping.

ME: Did you know that Frank played football?

K.L.: God, you're an ugly woman! Ugghh! All right, all right Gelman! I know, I know! It's time for Millennium Trivia.

ME: Did I show you these pictures?

K.L.: Yes, you showed the pictures, all right?

[The contestant on the phone—Marilyn—says she's a nutritionist]

ME: Reege, you're watching your diet, aren't you?

K.L.: Yeah. Watch this! Do you want to read the question?

ME: Can I, Reege? OH, THANK YOU!!! This is for Sondheim! Hey, Marilyn, do you have children? I want to send you my lullaby album. I can't get rid of the damn things!

K.L.: How many of those did you sell?

ME: Well, we sold about three—but I've given away five thousand.

THE FINAL INSULT

All right, I thought I was finished with this book, but here's one more story you probably ought to hear. Let's go back to the night Kathie Lee and I made our big final concert appearance together at Westbury Music Fair. This was the week before our last *Live!* broadcast together. So the concert was everything you would imagine it to have been. And, by that, I mean—

YES, SHE CRIED!

Before it was over, there were tears in the eyes of the three thousand excited people in the audience, too.

I even sang these special lyrics to "Thanks For The Memory" for her—

> *Thanks for the memory.*
> *You've been a lifelong pal,*
> *Boosted my morale,*
> *Got me and Joy a hefty discount cruising Carnival—*
> *The room was . . .*
> *Small.*

Thanks for the memory.
Your smile was always sunny.
You've made a lot of money.
You've come a long way since you were just a Hee Haw *Honey—*
And met Mr. Football.

Now comes a time when we're partin'.
After fifteen years, that's an option.
We'll put Gelman up for adoption.
But don't lose heart—
There's still Wal-Mart.

And thanks for the memory.
They said it wouldn't last.
Sure has been a blast.
We never won the Emmy, but we never were outclassed—
To the voters, kiss my—

Anyway, it was a wonderful show—adoration from the crowd, laughs, tears, everything. Afterward, there was a little party and then Joy and I got into the limo they had provided for us to get back to the city. Now, the ride back to Manhattan at that time of night still takes an hour. And because Joy had come up to Westbury just before show-time, she'd had no chance to eat all night. As it turned out, we didn't roll back into the city until nearly one o'clock in the morning.

So, as we were driving over the bridge into town, I knew it was coming—I knew there was going to be another stop before I got to bed. Right on cue, that's when Joy said, "Gee, I haven't eaten anything." At that hour, there aren't many options. So I said, "How about good old Gray's Papaya for a hot dog?" I had the limo driver take us up to the Gray's at Seventy-second and Broadway. I figured that I'd hop out, grab her hot dog, and be back in a minute.

Now, at one o'clock in the morning—after leaving that adoring throng of three thousand people—here I am standing around with the late-night grunge guys who are just settling in for their after-party hot dogs. I'm still wearing the ruffled tux shirt and tie from the concert—and looking pretty much out of place.

Right away, I notice that two young guys are staring at me. They seem a little bit strung out, too. Finally, one of them says, "Hey, man, are you the limo guy? How much would it cost to run me up to Eighty-eighth Street?"

So I start to say, "Well, I've got my wife in the car . . ."

Then I realize this kid thinks I'm a limo driver for hire!!

And the more I talk, the bigger the kid's eyes are getting. And, believe me, these were big eyes to begin with!

He says, "Hey, man, you sound just like Regis Philbin!"

Okay, I didn't LOOK like Regis Philbin—

But I sounded like Regis Philbin!

But then he figures it out and says, "Oh my God, man, I love that *Millionaire* show!"

Just two hours earlier, I'd been onstage with all those ovations—and now I'm waiting in line for a hot dog with the cast of *West Side Story*! And they're all giving me *"Is-that-your-final-answer"* in every way they can think of—

"Is this your final sauerkraut and mustard, man?"

"Hey, man, do you want your final french fries with that?"

Next, I'm signing dozens of autographs on sheets of frankfurter wrapping paper.

AND ALL I WANTED WAS ONE STINKING HOT DOG—AND IT WASN'T EVEN FOR ME!

Twenty minutes later, I fight my way out of there.

Then the first kid calls after me—

"Hey, man, what about that ride to Eighty-eighth Street?"

HE STILL THINKS I'M A DRIVER FOR HIRE WHO ALSO HAPPENS TO HOST A NETWORK TELEVISION SHOW!

Finally, I jump into the car.

Joy gives me a look and says, "What took you so long?"

As usual, I tell her what I always tell her and will continue to tell her for the rest of my life:

"YOU DON'T WANT TO KNOW."

All Right, It's Time
TO PLAY . . .

WHO WANTS TO BE ME?

$100

With whom do I have the most sexual tension?

A. Kathie Lee
B. Gelman
C. My urologist
D. Jerry Seinfeld

$200

Larry King has referred to me as

A. Altoona Hello
B. National Treasure
C. His idol
D. Mr. Suspenderless

$300

On *The Late Show with David Letterman*, I'm reverently called

A. The Overcaffeinated Monkey
B. The Pantywaist Liar
C. The Show Saver
D. Joy Philbin's Husband

$500

Kathie Lee left *Live!* to

A. Start her own construction company
B. Costar in Cody's next movie
C. Escape the sexual tension with Gelman
D. Write the songs that make the whole world sing

$1,000

Before Joy and I were married, my mother told her

A. "He's very handy around the house."
B. "I raised him like a fine piece of crystal."
C. "Are you sure you want to do this?"
D. "The poorhouse is just around the corner."

$2,000

I don't own a cell phone, but I do own

A. An enema kit
B. The New York Yankees
C. The American Broadcasting Company
D. Many broken tennis rackets

$4,000

On Saturday afternoons in the fall, I like to

A. Download pictures of Jerry Seinfeld on my computer
B. Watch Notre Dame destroy their opponents
C. Fix things around the house
D. Think about the old days

$8,000

I'm not very handy, but I once

A. Installed a bug zapper
B. Turned off the lights all by myself
C. Carved a wine rack for Gelman
D. Chain-sawed an entire forest of new saplings

$16,000

My first car was

A. A Hudson convertible

B. An Edsel

C. A Jaguar

D. A horse-drawn carriage

$32,000

I received a terrible leg wound from

A. A foul ball

B. Smacking myself while ruining a tennis racket

C. Kicking my computer because it wouldn't open

D. Kathie Lee's high heels

$64,000

I'm afraid of

A. Coyote urine

B. Cell phones

C. Women's shoe sales

D. All of the above

$125,000

For Father's Day a couple of years ago, I received

A. A blender
B. A chain saw
C. A box of rubber gloves
D. Gelman's everlasting respect

$250,000

I once paid $200 for

A. An overdue video
B. Art Moore's cape
C. A worthless bracelet for Joy
D. A colonoscopy

$500,000

What item was I returning to Caldor when I was thwarted by a little girl?

A. A *Who Wants to Be a Millionaire* CD-rom
B. A mop
C. A broken dimmer switch
D. A Tim Allen hammer

$1,000,000

Who was not seated at our table during *Time* magazine's seventy-fifth anniversary party?

A. George Bush
B. Claudia Schiffer
C. Wendy Wasserstein
D. David Copperfield

Feeling Confident? Are You Sure?
FINAL ANSWERS

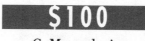

C. My urologist

B. National Treasure

C. The Show Saver

D. Write the songs that make the whole world sing

B. "I raised him like a fine piece of crystal."

D. Many broken tennis rackets

B. Watch Notre Dame destroy their opponents

B. Turned off the lights all by myself

A. A Hudson convertible

A. A foul ball

D. All of the above

A. A blender

C. A worthless bracelet for Joy

B. A mop

A. George Bush

Acknowledgments

C omedy, they say, is when dumb things happen to other people; tragedy is when those things happen to you. If that's true, I couldn't be happier to be able to provide so many laughs over the years with my stories of pain and humiliation. Now you have a whole book full of them! Go ahead and laugh. Go crazy. What do you care? I don't mind. Really.

Anyway, I would like to give special thanks to some of the people who helped FORCE ME TO RE-LIVE THESE AGGRAVATIONS ALL OVER AGAIN! (What did they care?) But I do appreciate all of their efforts, nevertheless:

My friend Bill Zehme—who first profiled me in *Esquire* magazine in 1994 and then helped to co-author my first book, *I'm Only One Man!*— came back to expertly guide me through this one, too. He's only one man as well—who (fortunately) happens to know this man a little too well. Also, his chief point man, Mike Thomas, did a terrific job in helping to bring wit and order to this project.

For their patience and fine editorial skills, thanks to Bob Miller, Mary Ellen O'Neill, David Lott, and Carrie Covert, all at Hyperion; and for additional editorial assistance in Chicago, to Sara Brant and Josh Schollmeyer. At Buena Vista: Mary Kellogg-Joslyn (as ever), Debbie

Dolins, Anita Lannin, Sandra Tommasetti, and Tanya Boonsukha. For use of their *Late Show* Top Ten Lists, many thanks to David Letterman, Maria Pope, and Rob Burnett—from their Show Saver.

At *Live!*, my assistant Pam Edmonds was perfectly invaluable as always. At William Morris, my friend and agent Jimmy Griffin seemed to think I needed to tell more stories while I was busy saving a network—but he's always there, being the Irish bulldog. And, of course, his Italian counterpart at William Morris, Kenny DiCamillo, with whom I've shared many hectic and happy hours on the road.

Then there's Gelman and his staff at *Live!*—the smallest, hardest-working staff in television history. Most have been with me for years and years, and I appreciate their talent and loyalty.

And, finally, I'm especially proud to share many of the pages in this book with the all-too-wise voices of three beautiful women who know me all-too-well—my daughters J.J. and Joanna and my wife Joy. Joy, of course, has been the brains and the beauty and the backbone of this family. Without her, who knows where we would be—and who knows how I would have ever survived most of the stories in this book. There's no one else quite like her. She and Joanna and J.J. and my other daughter, Amy, and my son, Dan, mean the world to me. I'm proud of them—and of what they have accomplished and will accomplish. I hope they think of me with a smile and, most importantly, with a laugh when remembering our years together and all we've been through.

Regardless of what you've read before this, it really has been a wonderful life and I'm a lucky guy to have them—and also to have all of you. Thanks, everybody.

AND, YES, THIS IS MY
FINAL PAGE!